Take Sides with the Truth

Take Sides with the Truth

The Postwar Letters of
John Singleton Mosby to
Samuel F. Chapman

Edited by Peter A. Brown

THE UNIVERSITY PRESS OF KENTUCKY

Publication of this volume was made possible in part by a grant
from the National Endowment for the Humanities.

Scholarly publisher for the Commonwealth,
serving Bellarmine University, Berea College, Centre College of Kentucky,
Eastern Kentucky University, The Filson Historical Society, Georgetown
College, Kentucky Historical Society, Kentucky State University, Morehead
State University, Murray State University, Northern Kentucky University,
Transylvania University, University of Kentucky, University of Louisville,
and Western Kentucky University.
All rights reserved.

Editorial and Sales Offices: The University Press of Kentucky
663 South Limestone Street, Lexington, Kentucky 40508–4008
www.kentuckypress.com

11 10 09 08 07   5 4 3 2 1

Library of Congress Cataloging-in-Publication Data

Mosby, John Singleton, 1833–1916.
 Take sides with the truth: the postwar letters of John Singleton Mosby to
Samuel F. Chapman / edited by Peter A. Brown.
   p. cm.
 Includes bibliographical references and index.
 ISBN-13: 978-0-8131-2427-8 (hardcover: alk. paper)
 ISBN-10: 0-8131-2427-1 (hardcover: alk. paper) 1. Mosby, John Singleton,
1833–1916—Correspondence. 2. Chapman, Samuel Forrer, 1838–1919—
Correspondence. 3. Soldiers—Confederate States of America—Correspondence.
4. Confederate States of America. Army—Biography. 5. United States—
History—Civil War, 1861–1865—Campaigns. 6. Confederate States of
America. Army. Virginia Cavalry Battalion, 43rd. 7. Lee, Robert E. (Robert
Edward), 1807–1870—Military leadership. 8. Gettysburg Campaign, 1863.
9. Stuart, Jeb, 1833–1864—Military leadership. I. Chapman, Samuel Forrer,
1838–1919. II. Brown, Peter A. III. Title.
 E467.1.M87A4 2007
 973.7'3092—dc22   2006037321

This book is printed on acid-free recycled paper meeting the requirements of the
American National Standard for Permanence in Paper for Printed Library Materials.

∞ ⊛

Manufactured in the United States of America.

 Member of the Association of
American University Presses

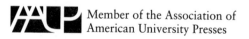

To Kitty,
who made it possible

"Tell him I say to take sides with the truth."
> —John Mosby to Sam Chapman,
> January 21, 1910

"I did not go for Phil (Sheridan) after Rosser's style, with a tomahawk & butcher knife, but shaved him with a sharp razor."
> —John Mosby to Sam Chapman,
> November 28, 1894

"I don't spare General Lee's staff officers—There was a lying concert between them. I mean Marshall, Long, & Taylor."
> —John Mosby to Sam Chapman,
> August 24, 1907

"I was only paying a small part of the debt owed you."
> —John Mosby to Sam Chapman,
> June 9, 1914

Contents

Foreword by Jeffry D. Wert   xi

Preface   1

Acknowledgments   7

Forged in Fire:
The Friendship of John Mosby
and Sam Chapman   9

THE LETTERS   19

Conclusion   155

Bibliography   157

Index   161

Foreword

John Singleton Mosby was, in the words of an acquaintance, "a disturbing companion." Mosby could be ill-tempered, cantankerous, obstinate, and brusque. He did not welcome disagreement with his views and glared with an icy look at men with whom he was displeased or who had failed him. There was a sharp edge and hard realism to him.

It was such a man who organized and commanded the Forty-third Battalion of Virginia Cavalry or Mosby's Rangers. With a keen intellect, an absolute fearlessness, and an unbending will, Mosby molded and disciplined hundreds of young bloods into the most effective partisan ranger command of the Civil War. For twenty-six months, from the winter of 1863 to the spring of 1865, Mosby's Rangers conducted guerrilla operations in northern Virginia, the Shenandoah Valley, and into Maryland. With the end of the Confederacy at hand, Mosby disbanded his command rather than surrender it to Union authorities.

In all, roughly 2,100 men served as Mosby's Rangers during the existence of the command. Hundreds spent a few weeks in the battalion; hundreds more, several months; and scores, from the earliest days to the end. Men such as Willie Foster, William Thomas Turner, Fount Beattie, Richard Montjoy, Dolly and Tom Richards, John Russell, and William and Samuel Chapman rose through the ranks and assumed leadership roles and company command in the battalion. Each man had been handpicked by Mosby.

When the Forty-third Battalion disbanded at Salem (now Marshall), Virginia, on April 21, 1865, the Rangers obtained paroles and returned to civilian life. It would be another thirty years before the surviving Rangers held a reunion, the only gathering Mosby attended. Their former commander, however, kept in touch with many of them while serving in government posts in Hong Kong and Washington, D.C., and as an attorney with a railroad in San Francisco.

Mosby enjoyed a close friendship with one of his finest officers, Samuel Chapman. Peter A. Brown, author of an excellent biography of Chapman, has gathered eighty-four postwar letters, spanning more than three decades, from Mosby to Chapman. Most of the letters have never been published before and offer a revealing portrait of Mosby, both as a man and as a former soldier. Although he could still be a "disturbing companion," Mosby demonstrates in these letters his loyalty and warmth to friends. This correspondence, ably edited and annotated by Mr. Brown, is most welcome.

Jeffry D. Wert
Centre Hall, Pennsylvania

Preface

John Singleton Mosby had practiced law in Bristol, Virginia, for nearly five years when, in the summer of 1860, the twenty-seven-year-old attorney was persuaded to join a newly formed cavalry company.[1] The following April the country found itself rendered asunder by civil war, and the new recruits were soon incorporated into the First Virginia Cavalry, commanded by Col. J. E. B. Stuart. Within a year Mosby became a scout for Stuart, who by that time had been promoted to brigadier general. In the late winter of 1862–1863, Stuart gave his determined scout the opportunity to gather and lead an independent partisan command.[2]

Samuel Forrer Chapman, a twenty-two-year-old ministerial student at Richmond College, left school and in May 1861 enlisted as a private in the Warren Rifles at Front Royal, Virginia. A month later the Warren Rifles became Company B of the Seventeenth Regiment, Virginia Infantry. That October Sam transferred to the Dixie Artillery, a Page County company, which his younger brother, William, a former student at the University of Virginia, helped to organize. Sam served as first lieutenant in the battery when William became commander. A year later, with the reorganization of General Lee's Army of Northern Virginia, the Dixie Artillery was disbanded, and the two brothers became enrollment and conscription officers in Warrenton, the county seat of Fauquier County, Virginia.[3]

In March 1863, Sam and William Chapman joined John Mosby and his fledgling partisan command. In July 1864, Sam, who had been serving as adjutant, was promoted to captain, in command of the newly formed Company E of the Forty-third Battalion. His brother William commanded Company C before becoming lieutenant colonel, second-in-command of the battalion, under Colonel Mosby.[4]

1

Gen. Robert E. Lee surrendered the Army of Northern Virginia at Appomattox Court House on April 9, 1865; on April 21, Colonel Mosby disbanded the Forty-third in lieu of surrender, and the following day Sam and William Chapman were paroled at Winchester, Virginia. John Mosby suffered nearly a year of harassment and arrests at the hands of Federal authorities before finally being paroled in February 1866, upon orders of Gen. U. S. Grant.[5]

After the war, Sam Chapman returned to his ministry in northern Virginia. He also worked, along with William, as a mail agent on the Railroad Mail Service, a position obtained with the assistance of John Mosby, who had become friends with President Grant.[6] Sam later served as superintendent of schools in Fauquier and Alleghany Counties, as well as postmaster in Covington, Virginia, and deputy U.S. marshal in Staunton, Virginia. In 1898–1899, he donned the blue uniform of the U.S. Army and served in Cuba as chaplain of the Fourth Regiment, U.S. Volunteer Infantry.[7] William Chapman eventually received an appointment as agent with the Internal Revenue Service. John Mosby practiced law in Warrenton and Washington, D.C.,[8] before becoming U.S. consul to Hong Kong. He worked as an attorney for the Southern Pacific Railroad in San Francisco, as a land agent for the U.S. Department of the Interior, and finally as an attorney in the U.S. Department of Justice in Washington, D.C. Sam Chapman remained a close confidant of Colonel Mosby, and the two exchanged correspondence and visited often in the ensuing years.

In 1914 John Mosby wrote to Sam Chapman concerning the practice of patronage in government positions: "I did have you appointed under Grant although you had not voted for him; nor did I consider it an act of generosity on my part as *I was only paying a small part of the debt owed you*" (emphasis added).[9] Mosby was referring to Sam's appointment as mail agent, in the patronage-heavy Railroad Mail Service, by President Grant.

Mosby's consideration of a "debt" owed by him to Chapman revealed, in a single word, the extent of the relationship between these two old veterans. Surely Sam Chapman had not performed any service for John Mosby since the war that would have Mosby think he had incurred a debt. He could only have been referring to what had taken place during the conflict when Sam served as one of Mosby's Rangers.

Midway through the war Mosby acquired a small howitzer, for use in raiding the railroads, and Sam was placed in charge of the weapon. In May 1863, Chapman used the cannon in an attack on a Union train near Catlett's Station, Virginia. It became apparent to Mosby that his force was badly outnumbered and Union cavalry would overtake them. Mosby told Sam to find a position for the small cannon where it would "exact all it was worth in blood."[10] Chapman placed the gun at the dead end of an inclined, fenced-in road near the village of Greenwich and stayed by it until the ammunition was exhausted. He then used the gun's rammer, swinging it as a weapon until felled by a shot in the thigh.[11] His courage and fearless nature made it possible for Mosby and the others to escape while he lay wounded on the ground awaiting death or capture. Thus, it might be said a "debt" was incurred. This was but a single example; surely there were others during those memorable years of 1863–1865.

It is irrefutable that Mosby thought highly of Chapman. Following Sam's recovery from his near fatal wound, he was assigned to another command. A few months later, Mosby wrote to the secretary of war asking that Sam Chapman be returned to his command and promoted to adjutant, saying that he would "regard his appointment as a special favor."[12]

There were many more fights to come and many times when Sam Chapman, the preacher-turned-soldier, fearlessly exhibited the same courage he had shown at Greenwich—even being seriously wounded again less than two years later. A comrade in the command said of him: "He was the bravest man I ever knew."[13]

That John Mosby was a copious writer is undeniable. The letters that he and Chapman exchanged easily number in excess of a hundred; the same can be said of Mosby's correspondence with other confidants, such as Fount Beattie, John Russell, and Ben Palmer.[14] Sam's son Willie, whom Mosby considered as his own,[15] and Sam's brother William—always referred to by Mosby as "Col. William"—were regular recipients of letters from the voluble writer. When considering the letters he wrote to family, especially to grandsons Mosby and Spottswood Campbell and daughters Ada and Stuart, it is difficult to fathom the number of lines he was able to put on paper, even after reaching the seventh and eighth decades of his life.

Aside from the number of letters, the feelings he was able to communicate and exhibit through writing were themselves remarkable. This was especially discernible in letters to Sam Chapman. At times he was as a fastidious teacher, such as when he cautioned Sam to return an item or not to lose one he had sent: "As I have no answer from you I fear you have lost it—although I warned you not to lose it."[16] He was still the "commander" decades after the war, when he wrote Sam relative to the group paintings to be done by a New York artist: "I want Fount to go with Colonel William. . . . It won't do for Dolly & Col. William to go together—they don't love each other."[17] In one instance he encouraged Sam to see President Wilson about a postmaster appointment: "I suggest you go there & call on him. You need to ask him to keep you on or put your son-in-law in. But, *incidentally*, you could tell him who you *are* and as well who you *were*." Another time he wanted Sam to apply for a chaplain position in the army: "Now the thing for you to do is to go to Washington and get the appointment as Chaplain to a regiment. . . . Go to my friend Judge Watson & show him this letter."[18]

The following letters cover a period of over thirty-five years—from 1880 to 1916. They are not intended to be a complete rendering of the correspondence from John Mosby to Sam Chapman. That there are other letters is a known fact, but their availability is either nil or questionable. The letters herein begin in Hong Kong, where Mosby was U.S. consul, and end in a Washington, D.C. hospital, where he was a patient, seven weeks before his death. They were all addressed to "Capt. Sam Chapman" in either Covington, Virginia, where Chapman served at various times as a Baptist preacher, school superintendent, and postmaster, or in Staunton, Virginia, where he was a deputy U.S. marshal. In a few instances letters to Sam Chapman's son Willie are included and reflect the paternalistic affection that Mosby felt for the boy.

Each of the reproduced letters in this volume is presented verbatim—exactly as written by Mosby, although the handwriting was difficult to decipher in several instances. Mosby was known to use sardonic quips repeatedly against those who had fallen into disfavor with him, and this was reflected in several letters. But his use of the language and his quotations from published works were remarkable and reveal a very literate and knowledgeable writer.

The great majority of the letters have only recently been made available to the general populace, and those few that were heretofore available are, for the first time, presented in their entirety.

1. Mosby, *Memoirs*, 11–12. Mosby says in his memoirs that it was William Blackford, later to be an officer on General Stuart's staff, who was helping organize the company.

2. Ibid., 30, 31, 106, 110, 148–49.

3. Brown, *Mosby's Fighting Parson*, 35–36, 81–82, 89, 90; Virginia Baptist Historical Society, Richmond; National Archives (NA), Washington, D.C.; Compiled Service Records of the Union and the Confederacy (CSR), Seventeenth Virginia Infantry. William H. Chapman was lieutenant and then captain of the Dixie Artillery before joining Mosby's command.

4. Brown, *Mosby's Fighting Parson*, 141, 192; Mosby, *Memoirs*, 390–91; NA, CSR, Forty-third Battalion, Virginia Cavalry; Virginia Baptist Historical Society. William Chapman, although a lieutenant colonel, was always referred to as "Col. William" in Mosby's postwar letters to Sam Chapman.

5. Brown, *Mosby's Fighting Parson*, 290, 291–92; Mosby, *Memoirs*, 390–91.

6. Brown, *Mosby's Fighting Parson*, 298, 299–300; *Alexandria Gazette*, June 9, 1873; *Washington Times*, April 23, 1894.

7. NA, Record Group 094, Regimental Returns Fourth U.S. Volunteers, Spanish War; Brown, *Mosby's Fighting Parson*, 297, 317–18, 323, 325, 341, 345.

8. Mosby, *Memoirs*, passim; Brown, *Mosby's Fighting Parson*, passim.

9. GLC 3921.46. John Mosby. Autograph letter signed: to Sam Chapman, 9 June 1914 (The Gilder Lehrman Collection, courtesy of The Gilder Lehrman Institute of American History, New York).

10. Mosby, *Mosby's War Reminiscences*, 146 (facsimile reprint edition, 1995).

11. Ibid., 148–50.

12. Brown, *Mosby's Fighting Parson*, 134–35.

13. Wert, *Mosby's Rangers*, 184.

14. Fountain "Fount" Beattie, John Singleton Russell, and William Benjamin "Ben" Palmer were all lieutenants in either Sam's or William's company during the war. They were close friends with both Mosby and Sam. John Russell was Mosby's favorite scout and after the war took his commander's middle name (Singleton) as his own.

15. Mewborn Collection, Letter from John Mosby to Sam Chapman, ca. 1899.

16. GLC 3921.51. John Mosby. Autograph letter signed: to Sam Chapman, 18 June 1915 (The Gilder Lehrman Collection, courtesy of The Gilder Lehrman Institute of American History, New York).

17. GLC 3921.49. John Mosby. Autograph letter signed: to Sam Chap-

man, 4 February 1915 (The Gilder Lehrman Collection, courtesy of The Gilder Lehrman Institute of American History, New York).

18. GLC 3921.44. John Mosby. Autograph letter signed: to Sam Chapman, 19 April 1914 (The Gilder Lehrman Collection, courtesy of The Gilder Lehrman Institute of American History, New York); Judge Walter Allen Watson was a former member of the Virginia senate, circuit court judge, and U.S. congressman.

Acknowledgments

The initial idea for this work came out of conversations with an individual I have yet to meet face-to-face but have come to know as a friend and fellow traveler along the road of Civil War history. Joe Bauman of Salt Lake City is a veteran reporter for the *Deseret Morning News*. Following the publication of *Mosby's Fighting Parson: The Life and Times of Sam Chapman* (Willow Bend Books, 2001), I was put in touch with Joe, a collector of antique photographs, who has an image of Sam Chapman of which I was unaware. Through my conversation with Joe and correspondence from a Chapman descendant, I was made aware that The Gilder Lehrman Institute of American History in New York had cataloged several post–Civil War letters written by Col. John Mosby to Capt. (and Rev.) Sam Chapman. Using this information I was able to locate these letters, and they have become the heart and soul of this book.

My heartfelt thanks to Leslie Fields, associate curator for The Gilder Lehrman Collection, without whose help this work would certainly not have had life in its present form.

The Stuart-Mosby Historical Society was gracious enough to print copies of several letters from their archives. I am particularly thankful to Col. Ralph "Mitch" Mitchell (USA-Ret.) for his labors in this regard. Also, thanks go to Jackie Lee of the Fauquier Historical Society in Warrenton, Virginia, who, upon learning of my interest, loaned letters written by John Mosby's brother, Willie, to Sam Chapman.

Individuals who helped me in locating letters for my previous book on Sam Chapman were again helpful for this endeavor, including Horace Mewborn, Hugh Keen, and John Kincheloe. My thanks also to David Goetz, who transcribed and copied for me an engaging letter he had acquired.

Last, but in no way least, I owe to my wife, Kitty, the inspiration for this book. She believed that I could bring, through these letters, a new understanding of John Mosby, the man, not just the warrior, and also present to the reader a unique relationship that existed between two uncommon veterans—one an agnostic-leaning commander, now with no command, and the other a Baptist preacher and onetime subordinate, trying to find his place in postwar Virginia.

Forged in Fire

The Friendship of John Mosby
and Sam Chapman

Samuel Chapman was a former infantry private and artillery officer when he was assigned to enrollment duties in Fauquier County. And it was here, in January 1863, that the twenty-four-year-old lieutenant first saw John Mosby. Chapman had heard talk about Mosby and his daring exploits—or his foolhardy exploits, depending upon who was doing the talking—behind the Union lines, and he would hear more in the weeks to come. Less than two months after first seeing Mosby in Warrenton and hearing the stories being told in and around the court-house, Chapman joined Mosby and his young, still-developing band of Rangers. And when he spoke of his former duties, Chapman would say: "Finding it not at all to my taste, I asked to be relieved of gathering men who were very unwilling to leave their homes to become soldiers." This decision marked the beginning of a bond between the two Confederates that would weave and mold and shape itself over the next half century and culminate in a common respect and esteem that overcame vast differences in both temperament and doctrine. It would not end until Mosby's death in 1916. Three years later, nearly to the day of his friend's death, Rev. Sam Chapman would pass away.

Early on in his career as one of Mosby's Rangers, Sam Chapman came to appreciate Mosby's leadership and the power he had over his men. Even before the group was fully organized into a fighting machine, Chapman understood that the cohesion of this varied assortment of men relied on two things: One, "the love of adventure" and, two, "the confidence in their leader." And it would not take Mosby long to see just what kind of subordinate he had in Sam Chapman. Many years after the war, while he was living in San Francisco, Mosby's thoughts returned, as they often did, to that time long ago. On one such occasion he wrote to Sam back in Virginia: "I just wish you could be here with me, I wd. [would] feel as young as I was at Miskel's gate when I burst into laughing in the midst of the fight when I saw you standing in your stirrups whaling the Yankees with your sabre."

Chapman had been with Mosby for slightly over two months when Jeb Stuart sent the command a new weapon—a small mountain howitzer—that Mosby had requested for use in raiding the railroads. Acknowledging the confidence he had in Chapman, Mosby placed him in charge of the gun, gave him a crew of three, and after only one quick rehearsal, struck a Union supply train on the Orange & Alexandria Railroad near Catlett's Station. The result of this particular event was the loss of the gun and the severe wounding and capture of Chapman, but not without a gallant stand at Grapewood Farm, near Greenwich. Here, Chapman, after exhausting his ammunition, stood by the cannon, swinging the rammer at the enemy who surrounded him. Again Mosby characterized Chapman, showing once more how much he thought of his new comrade: "He was one of the noblest and most heroic soldiers in the Southern army. Sam had passed through so many fights unscathed that the men had a superstition that he was invulnerable. His hour had come at last and a bullet pierced the celestial armor of the solider-priest."

Following Chapman's recovery from the wounding at Greenwich, he was reassigned once more to an artillery unit. This was in July 1863, and that winter would find him in Petersburg assigned as a member of the courts-martial board in Pickett's Division. And again Mosby would convey his confidence in the former Ranger, writing a personal request to the Confederate secretary of war: "I respectfully request the appointment of Lieut. Samuel F. Chapman as Adjutant of this battalion. Lieut. Chapman was originally a lieutenant in an artillery company which was afterward consolidated with another. He was relieved of duty in his company and appointed to the Conscript bureau, then was assigned to Caskie's battery, Dearing's battalion, Pickett's Division. He has rendered valuable services with my command & I would regard his appointment as a personal favor." Mosby's request was immediately granted, and once more Sam was back with the Rangers, serving as the command's first adjutant.

On a day in July 1864, Mosby with about 150 Rangers met up with 250 troopers from the Second Massachusetts and Thirteenth New York Cavalries commanded by Maj. William H. Forbes. A fierce fight took place in a field and wood adjacent to the Little River Turnpike at Mt. Zion Church, about two miles east of the village of Aldie. Despite the bravery of the Union commander, Major Forbes, the Southerners were able to inflict a terrible carnage on their numerically larger enemy. The fight began when Sam Chapman fired a round from the Rangers' howitzer. This was followed by a charge into the Union front and flank, which drove the Federals back, first in confusion and then in a rout. The brave Major Forbes, his horse shot from underneath him, was finally forced to surrender what was left of his command. The carnage from the fight included seventeen Union dead and forty wounded—twelve to fifteen of these mortally. Counting the wounded who were taken prisoner, the Federals surrendered over one hundred men to the Rangers, including their commander, Major Forbes. Nearly fifty years later, Colonel Mosby recalled the fight in a letter to Sam Chapman's son Willie, saying, "One of my men took Maj. Forbes' watch when he was a prisoner. Your father took it from the man and gave it back to Forbes." Thus, so minor an incident nearly half a century before still had a revered place in the mind of the old commander when thoughts of his friend were affectionately aroused within him. Three weeks after the Mt. Zion fight, Mosby promoted Chapman to captain, in command of the newly formed Company E. He remembered Sam's venturing and courageous character, saying, "I made him a captain for it."

In September 1864, Captain Chapman took a contingent of the Rangers across the Blue Ridge to Front Royal, where he ordered an attack on what he thought was a two-hundred-man Yankee wagon train. It was, in fact, the whole Reserve Brigade of Union general Torbert's cavalry, and the debacle that followed would haunt those involved for the rest of their lives. Six of Chapman's men were captured and brutally executed by the Federals—four were shot and two were hanged. Colonel Mosby, on leave at the time after having been wounded the week before, returned to the command later that month. Instead of rebuking Chapman for what might have been construed as recklessness or worse, Mosby asked Chapman for his report of the affair. He then assembled the command and dispatched Chapman with his company into the Shenandoah Valley once more, this time to ascertain what Sheridan was up to and to disrupt his lines of communication. This single act served to show the rest of the command just what faith the commander had in his newest captain.

Following the execution of the six Rangers at Front Royal and another in Rappahannock County a few weeks later, Mosby had determined to reciprocate in kind. Believing that Custer was responsible for the atrocities, he ordered seven prisoners from Custer's command be executed as near to Custer's headquarters as possible. On a cold, rainy night in November 1864, a detail of the Rangers proceeded to carry out Mosby's orders. The contingent got to the vicinity of Berryville and felt that this was as close to Custer's camp in Winchester as they could safely go. The executions, while somewhat botched, took place. Years later, just prior to the thirty-fifth anniversary of the Front Royal affair, at which time a monument was to be dedicated to the six slain Rangers, Mosby wrote a letter to Chapman. In the letter Mosby disclosed, for the first time, the circumstances surrounding the retaliatory executions of Custer's men. Although General Lee and the Confederate War Department were made aware of what Mosby planned to do, he did not ask for their permission to do so. Mosby told Sam, "Take this letter with you & show it to the men & give them all my love." Mosby wrote that the letter would "for the first time . . . give to the world a true account of the Front Royal affair." He continued: "The world has never known that I reported it to Genl. Lee & that both he & Secretary Seddon not only approved but ordered me to do it. . . . You will see that my letter to Genl. Lee does not ask for instructions—it tells him what I was going to do & I did it. I have always kept it a secret that I had the order. I did not want to shirk responsibility for doing what I thought was right." The former leader added: "I never did anything that my conscience more thoroughly approved—that Torbert-Merritt-& Custer were ashamed of hanging my men is proved by their not alluding to it in their reports. My retaliation was a merciful act. It saved lives of both our men & the Yankees. The war wd. [would] have degenerated into a massacre." Again Colonel Mosby relied on his old friend to act for him concerning something he felt very strongly about.

Tom Richards was the older brother of Dolly Richards, and there existed a strong jealousy on the part of Tom who felt "mortified and embarrassed" because he had been passed over for promotion and his younger brother—younger by some fifteen years—consistently held rank over him. So in August 1864, Mosby detailed Tom Richards to the Northern Neck of Virginia to mobilize a force for the protection of the citizens there. The mission failed, and Richards was shortly thereafter back with the command.

For whatever faults he might have had, Tom Richards was a very brave soldier. He had been wounded three times and had also been captured, spending some time in Union prisons before being exchanged. And it was Tom Richards who had engaged in close combat with Union major Forbes at Mt. Zion Church and felt the pain of Forbes's saber in his shoulder. So it was general knowledge that Mosby had chosen Richards for the Northern Neck assignment because of his past heroics. However, it was revealed after the war that Mosby had ulterior reasons for sending Richards to the Northern Neck: he had done so at the suggestion of Sam Chapman. With confidence in Chapman's judgment, Mosby had chosen Richards not because of the widely accepted reasons but because Sam Chapman believed it best to have him away from the command for a time. Sam felt the rivalry and hard feelings Tom was displaying toward his younger brother were having a detrimental effect within the command.

The incidences and events I have related here occurred during the war or were based on events that took place during those years. But in the decades that followed, the relationship that had been borne of those times would continue to be molded into an ever tighter, stronger bond of mutual respect and esteem.

Following the end of hostilities, Mosby used his friendship with President Grant to secure patronage positions for several members of his old command. Sam Chapman was among these; twice, through Mosby's influence, Sam had been appointed to the Railway Postal Service.

The friendship of Mosby and Chapman was felt by the next generation of Chapmans as well. Sam's son Willie lived for several years in San Francisco, working as purser for a steamship company plying its trade between the California coast and the Far East. During part of this time, John Mosby was living in San Francisco also. The closeness of the relationship between the aging veteran and the young, handsome, and personable Willie is reflected in some of the letters Mosby wrote to Sam Chapman. In one instance he remarked how proud he was of the boy, calling him his "protégé," and saying that he knew Willie "would make his mark and be successful." He mentioned on more than one occasion the fact that Willie was Sam's son: "He is an apt scholar; in fact he does not need a teacher—is the son of his father!" And again: "That fighting son of yours is evidently a son of his father." He later told Sam of his efforts to help Willie obtain a promotion: "I went to see the superintendent about putting Willie a peg higher. He is a splendid boy—everybody takes a liking to him." Even on a social basis the deep friendship is evident: "[Willie] always comes straight to my room as soon as he lands. I feel toward him as if he were my son," Mosby wrote. In another letter, the Colonel shares details of a social outing with the young Chapman: "I took him to see some ladies last night. I got sleepy & came home—left Willie with them!"

Over the years that followed the two men exchanged much correspondence. And the Colonel visited with his old captain several times at Sam's home in Covington. But as the Reverend Chapman seemed to mellow and grow more humble with the passing years, the aging colonel appeared to become more cynical. He became more critical in his evaluations of persons and situations, and at times it was most difficult to separate his sardonic attitude from his biting humor. And John Mosby's own sensitivity seemed to grow diametrically in proportion to his criticism of others. Sam Chapman was not spared.

Upon the publication in 1896 of former Ranger James J. Williamson's book, *Mosby's Rangers*, Mosby wrote to Chapman saying, "Your picture in the volume does not suggest the idea of a minister of the Peace." And following the end of the Spanish-American War, in which Sam had served as chaplain with a volunteer infantry regiment, Mosby encouraged him to apply for a chaplain's commission with the American forces heading to the Philippines. "An ocean voyage will help you," he wrote. "There will be little exposure and if the climate doesn't suit, will be easy enough to get a furlough and come home (invalid), drawing a salary all the time." This reference to Sam's being "invalid" apparently refers to the effects of the malaria he had contracted while in Cuba. It appears that Mosby was suggesting to Sam that he could adopt a state of malingering if the proposed position was not suitable. This is difficult to accept in a person as moral and ethical as the Colonel; so, the inference may have been made in jest. Or had Mosby's cynicism began to impact upon his normally impeccable principles?

With Sam's son Willie already established in San Francisco, a second son, Elgin, was leaving home for the same destination. In a letter to Willie, Sam put in an aside to his friend: "Tell the Col. that his friends are still a trouble to him, but I know his little colony out there will be a comfort and perhaps a joy to him. I'll speak for their fidelity to him. Give our love to the Col. and them all."

Rebecca Chapman had grown seriously ill soon after her husband's return from Cuba. Now terminally ill with Bright's disease, she died on December 2, 1900, at the age of fifty-six. On the very day of her death, Sam took pen and wrote to John Mosby: "We are in the deepest affliction. When you come in stop and see us. The presence of a friend is a great comfort to us all and no one would console more than yourself." Sam continued on in much the same vein and then, knowing that Mosby would be the one to inform Willie, who was at sea, of his mother's death, closed with: "How distressed poor Willie will be. Good night my dear Colonel and may God bless you and yours is the prayer of your unworthy friend."

Just as the two friends could console each other in times of need, they could also display a sterner side when the situation called for it. Sam was after Mosby and his friend and fellow veteran Senator John Daniel to find a place for him in the federal government. Fount Beattie, Chapman's former lieutenant in Company E, had written to Sam saying that Sam might be able to get a storekeeper's position with the government. Sam then wrote to Mosby, referring to Beattie's suggestion and saying that Beattie's "mind must be in a state of eclipse" to suggest such a thing. John Mosby's reply was scathing. It revealed just why Mosby would get so upset with Chapman's response to Beattie's storekeeper's recommendation and detailed Mosby's disdain for the patronage system he had long been a partner in: "I have no idea of mingling anymore in controversies over patronage. I wish I never had. In justice to Fount I ought to say that I first suggested to him to write you & make the offer." In closing, Mosby reproved his old subordinate for believing a storekeeper's job was too menial for him: "Pulling down fences," he wrote, referring to his former position with the

Department of Land Management in the West, "is not as dignified as arguing cases in the Supreme Court. I have done both." In an earlier letter, Mosby, apparently thinking Chapman was not applying himself fully in seeking employment with the government, rebuked him: "I am sure you can get a place if you will only rouse yourself and try. (Take a few lessons in that sort of tact & skill from Colonel William and Josie)," he wrote, referring to Sam's brother and sister-in-law.

In writing to Sam Chapman, Colonel Mosby did not conceal his disdain for some of the former Rangers, either. Sam was living in Staunton, serving as a deputy U.S. marshal, when he joined the local Camp of the United Confederate Veterans. Among the members was a local businessman and former comrade in both the Seventeenth Virginia Infantry and the Forty-third Battalion, Hugh McIlhany. Hugh had joined the Forty-third in September 1864 after serving as chief quartermaster for General Longstreet's First Army Corps. His service as a Ranger was short-lived. He was captured after serving slightly over three months in the battalion. In a speech at the 1906 reunion of the Rangers, McIlhany had reminisced about the war and the hardships he had endured. Mosby had apparently read the remarks in the newspaper for he wrote to Sam alluding to them: "I was amused at Hugh's speech. . . . I don't suppose Hugh suffered much in the Commissary Dept. where he was until he joined our command. Don't think he could have suffered much in the three months he was with us but the report says his recital of his hardships drew tears. (I wd. [would] have laughed.) . . . It was during the time Hugh was with us that we made the greenback raid. . . . I have no doubt that Hugh had a stomach full when he was captured—probably had some greenbacks."

The Colonel did not spare Syd Ferguson from his biting criticisms either. Ferguson, while a young eighteen-year-old Ranger, had pursued and captured Capt. Richard Blazer, leader of the scouts of the same name, by hitting him over the head with the butt of his revolver during the fight at Myerstown in November 1864. Following the war, Ferguson enrolled in college and later seminary and became an ordained minister in the Methodist Church. When the first Ranger reunion was held in Alexandria in January 1895, Ferguson had written that he could not come "for fear several souls would be lost if he left [Fredericksburg]." Mosby was not pleased that Ferguson had not attended the reunion, and he was still thinking about it eight months later when he wrote to Chapman: "I think the Reverend Sid [sic] might have left the mourners one night to attend the reunion. I never could see the sense of people's mourning at the prospect of going to Heaven." And reminiscent of what he would later say about Sam Chapman, Mosby concluded: "I suspect Sid [sic] could send (& has sent) more people to Heaven by shooting at them than by preaching." (Incidentally, this reunion was the only one of these events Mosby would ever attend.)

Despite his apparent cynical view of the world, at times John Mosby ironically showed an entirely different side of his complex character. A year after losing his position at the Justice Department, "kicked out" as he called it, he wrote young Willie Chapman just after returning from an extended trip: "Much to my surprise a bank sent me a check to pay for my expenses on the excursion. It was a contribution from friends. . . . All of which proves the truth of what I have often said that the world is growing better every day." He then added an aside for Willie's father, Sam: "Of course a lot of pretty girls showed their affection for me and I wish that Reverend Sam had been there to enjoy the distribution of favors." This risqué exchange of a sort continued when Sam replied to Mosby, expressing his concern for his continued appointment as postmaster in Covington: "Well I shall not cry nor beg . . . I am thankful I am in good health. My kindest regards to the ladies. I would like to see them again."

On at least one occasion, in his correspondence with Mosby, Chapman revealed an uncharacteristic side of the now gentle and mellow minister. Henry Stuart was Jeb Stuart's nephew and was soon to be the next Virginia governor. But he had found disfavor with Mosby for his failure to speak up in his uncle's defense while Mosby was defending Jeb against critics for his actions at Gettysburg. In a letter to Mosby, Sam had written: "I was much pleased with your letter to Henry Stuart. He must be of different metal [sic] from his great kinsman. The older I get the less I like 'jelly fish' people. I meet every day people of more ability & learning than I have and yet of so little moral courage that I do not care to stay around them."

Ella Lee Chapman was the eldest child of Sam and Rebecca. She was born in 1866 and, never marrying, lived with her father until his death in 1919. She died in 1954 at the age of eighty-eight. Ella well remembered the visits by Colonel Mosby to the Chapman home, and she put down on paper some of her remembrances in later life. "The old veterans would come to the house and the most frequent visitor among them was Col. Mosby. He and my father would sit and discuss for hours the bygone actions and occurrences of the Civil War. They seemed to dwell in the Colonel's mind. He would draw diagrams on any scrap of paper at hand. Even his letters to my father when they were separated were full of references to the war. These letters came very often, as long as he lived, for he and my father were close friends."

The relationship between John Mosby and Sam Chapman can best be evaluated by a letter Mosby wrote to Sam in 1894, when the then-sixty-one-year-old veteran was planning a trip from California to see Sam in Covington. Asking Chapman to make the train connections for him he said: "I would prefer to reach there in the daytime or early in the night," he confided, "as I have a *horror* of being waked up at night." I have no reservation in saying that I do not believe John Mosby ever made such a candid personal acknowledgment to any other person.

Source: previously published in the April 2002 issue of *Southern Cavalry Review.*

The Letters

Hong Kong—1880

Col. John Mosby served as U.S. consul in the British Crown Colony of Hong Kong, having been appointed to the position by President Hayes in early 1879. By the following year he longed for a furlough to return to see his motherless children. But probably due to his revelations of corruption in the consulate service, as well as in the State Department, members of the administration did not want him back in the United States, where he would be available to the press—and to Congress. Hayes, keenly aware of the political firestorm Mosby could ignite if allowed to come home, was in agreement. Mosby was quite anxious about his fate as he awaited the coming election between his friend James Garfield and the Democrat Winfield Scott Hancock. His close friend Sam Chapman worked as head postal clerk on the railway postal run between Washington, D.C., and Charlotte, North Carolina, having given up his pastorate at Woodlawn Baptist Church near Alexandria.

<hr />

Sept 20th, 1880   United States Consulate
Captain S. F. Chapman   Hong Kong

Dear Sam:

I enclose a piece I have written about Hancock in which I make a point against him that I have never made. I wd. like for you to get Forbes or someone else to publish. Forbes can substitute "Courtland Smith" for "Mayor of Alex [andria] if he wishes.[1] I have no idea that he wd. consider such a thing if it were to occur, as either a calamity or a crime. Write me a long letter as soon as the election is over & give me all the local news. I hope to see you in a few months—that much I think is certain if I live. If Garfield is elected I want to start

21

home in time to be at the inauguration—if Hancock is elected I shall send in my resignation so as to reach there by that time. Hancock personally might be willing for me to remain here but he will be in the hands of his party friends. If Hunton—Genl. Smith—Genl. Payne—&c.[2]—demand my dismissal, as they wd. have a perfect right to do on party grounds, then Hancock wd. be bound to do it. If he does not do it & they do not request it, then it wd. be said that my remaining in office was due to the forbearance of Hunton &c. and I do not intend to be even that much in their debt. I don't intend to have anything by their influence. If I have to go down, I intend to die like Lochiel—"with my back to the field and my face to my foes."[3] This is my motto & I want you to let everyone who takes any interest in me know it. I have been thinking in the event of Garfield's election you might be my successor at Hong Kong—think of it. I see that Brooke[4] in a speech at Warrenton says "all true Virginians" were for Hancock—so they were for Grant & Tilden but mighty anxious to get a few crumbs from Grant & Hayes. How humble they will be if Garfield is elected, but I do not intend to eat humble pie—how arrogant if Hancock is. I hope "the statesman" will not turn our friend [illegible] out of his P.O.

Yours truly
Jno. S. Mosby[5]

James Garfield won the election and in July 1881 approved a furlough for Mosby. However, a few days later, an assassin's bullet mortally wounded the new president and Mosby's long wished for furlough was lost in the chaos that followed.[6] Garfield died in September 1881, and Mosby was destined to remain in Hong Kong throughout the term of Garfield's successor, Chester A. Arthur. Mosby was replaced as consul after the Democratic administration of President Grover Cleveland took office, and he finally left Hong Kong in late July 1885.

1. Courtland Smith was mayor of Alexandria, Virginia, 1878–1881.
2. Faust, *Encyclopedia of the Civil War*. Gen. Winfield Scott Hancock, a Union hero, was the Democratic standard-bearer in the election of 1880.

Eppa Hunton and William "Extra Billy" Smith were Confederate generals in the war; Smith was a two-term Virginia governor; Hunton and Alexander D. F. Payne were Warrenton lawyers.

3. Thomas Campbell, *Lochiels' Warning*, ca. 1808. Actual quote is: "With his back to the field and his feet to the foe."

4. James V. Brooke Jr. was a Warrenton attorney and served as court commissioner.

5. John T. Kincheloe Collection.

6. Siepel, *Rebel*, 231.

Contempt for Tom Richards

Following his return from Hong Kong, Mosby was employed as an attorney with the Southern Pacific Railroad and took up quarters in San Francisco. Sam Chapman had moved with his family to Covington, Virginia, having accepted a calling to the Baptist church there. Sam's second son, William—known affectionately as "Willie"—relocated to San Francisco following a stint at the University of Virginia. He was only one of several relations of former Rangers to migrate west; many found work thanks to the generous influence of Mosby. They would be known, in Mosby's vernacularism, as the "aborigines."[1] Far and away the favorite of the Colonel was Willie Chapman.

———————

Sept. 6th/94   1002 A Bank St., S.F.

Dear Sam—

I rec'd your letter over a week ago & forwarded it to my daughter Stuart[2] who is spending the summer at Fairfax C. H. I sent you a copy of *The Call* with the account of my being wounded at old Lud Lake's.[3] I had a particular object in publishing this to show that I was shot after having been taken prisoner. I did this not to reproach anyone but to show that acts of carelessness are often committed in war & peace, for wch. those in authority cannot be held responsible—besides I have always felt grateful to them for shooting me. If some man of our command had done this the whole command wd. have been denounced as a set of cut-throats. Willie was to see me last night looking very well. The purser in his ship has resigned

& this puts Willie a degree nearer the coveted position in the O&O Co.[4] They are promoted (if efficient) according to seniority. I went to see the Superintendent about putting Willie a peg higher but he said that although Willie is a great favorite his time hasn't come yet. There are two ahead of him. He has a very nice place now, no expenses except for his clothes. He told me that he was going to see his girl this evening but will call by my room on the way. I sent Tom Richards[5] a personal slip with my article & asked him to give it to the Los Angeles papers as I have a great many friends there who wd. like to see it. I supposed he felt some pride in Major Dolly (although I know he was very jealous of him) but I thought he wd. like on that account to see it published. He didn't take the least notice of my letter. I have often heard of his saying how mortifying it was to him to be in a command where a younger brother was a senior officer. For that reason (at your suggestion, I think) I sent him to the Northern Neck.[6] A year or so ago in Los Angeles he complained to me that Dolly had done him injustice in the Blazer fight.[7] As I have always heard full justice done him & had never heard of Dolly's doing him injustice, it rather gave me contempt for him. You are in the same situation in regard to your brother William but I wd. not have a very high opinion of you if I were to hear of your making such a speech. It was purely accidental both in your's & Tom's case that your elder[8] brothers got ahead of you. I have no doubt but that you were gratified at it. A good many papers published my first articles (including the *Cincinnati Gazette*) I have another out on Sunday Sept. 16th. I hope I see you on my next trip East. Love to your wife.

Yours Sincerely
Jno. S. Mosby[9]

In the August 19, 1894, edition of the *Morning Call*, Colonel Mosby related the events surrounding his most serious wound of the war, which occurred in December 1864. The shot that struck him was fired from outside the house of his friend Ludwell Lake. It entered through the glass of a closed window, striking Mosby in the stomach. As Mosby recalled: "A Northern officer was standing near talking to me when I was shot. Although I was a prisoner at the time I never complained of it for it was a lucky shot."[10] In August 1864 Mosby dispatched Tom Richards to the Northern Neck. General Lee, at Secretary of War Seddon's urging, had asked Mosby to recommend someone who could be sent there to mobilize and train a local force for defense from incursions by Union forces. Lee was less inclined than Seddon to send the troops because he felt there were men on the Neck that should be in the regular army but were not. Lee finally gave in to the secretary and Mosby in turn saw the opportunity, at Sam Chapman's suggestion, to separate Tom from his brother Dolly and the rest of the command to alleviate the bickering.[11]

1. GLC 3921.13. John Mosby. Autograph letter signed: to Sam Chapman, 20 January 1906 (The Gilder Lehrman Collection, courtesy of The Gilder Lehrman Institute of American History, New York).

2. Ramage, *Gray Ghost*, 319. Virginia Stuart (Mosby) Coleman did freelance writing.

3. Keen and Mewborn, *43rd Battalion*, 339, 340; Ludwell Lake lived near Rector's Cross Roads, Virginia. He had two sons who rode with Mosby's command.

4. The Occidental and Oriental Steamship Co. operated between San Francisco and Japan/China; Willie Chapman, Sam's son, served on one of the firm's ships.

5. Keen and Mewborn, *43rd Battalion*, 360, 361. Thomas W. Richards was the older brother of Maj. A. E. "Dolly" Richards; both men served as officers in the Forty-third Battalion, Mosby's command.

6. The Northern Neck of Virginia is a narrow peninsula lying between the Potomac and Rappahannock Rivers in eastern Virginia.

7. Brown, *Mosby's Fighting Parson*, 216, 219, 257–59; Keen and Mewborn, *43rd Battalion,* 361. In the late summer of 1864 the Blazer Scouts, a select group of one hundred Union cavalrymen, armed with the new Spencer repeating rifles, was organized on Gen. Philip Sheridan's order to "clean out Mosby's gang." Following some success against Mosby, the Scouts were nearly annihilated a few months later by Mosby's partisans led by Dolly Richards. Tom Richards received a promotion to captain ten days later.

8. Mosby obviously intended to say younger, not elder.

9. Peter A. Brown Collection.

10 *San Francisco Morning Call,* August 19, 1894.

11. Brown, *Mosby's Fighting Parson*, 260.

"The Solid South Is Broken"

The nineteenth century's deepest depression overran the nation in 1894, having its beginnings in the Panic of 1893. Grover Cleveland returned to office as president in 1894, after serving a previous term between 1885 and 1889, but the Democratic figurehead was powerless to stop the runaway economic train with its four million unemployed workers and the treasury being drained of its gold reserve by nervous European investors selling their American bonds.[1] Colonel Mosby was nearly gleeful as he envisioned the Democratic "Solid South" losing its political power.

———⊙———

Nov. 12th [1894]   1002 Bush St., S.F.

Dear Sam—

The Belgic[2] arrived a few days ago—Willie is here looking very well. I took him to see some ladies last night. I got sleepy & came home—left him with them. What a deluge!!! The democrats can't recover from it before the next presidential election. The Solid South is broken.[3] I start east December 1st, via Ogden to see Bev—Denver to see Johnnie. Will stop at Louisville with Captain Dolly[4]—at Covington to see Captain Sam. Sometime ago I wrote an account of the Blazer fight—sent ms: [manuscript] to my daughter Stuart. She writes me that it will be published in *Harper's Weekly*—maybe it is already out. I expect Captain Dolly will buy out the whole edition for distribution. Did you see my article in the *Dispatch*—"*Romance of War.*"[5] I wrote to Colonel Chapman & asked him to come on to Washington. Give my love to your wife.

Sincerely yours
Jno. S. Mosby[6]

———⊙———

The "Solid South" term is attributed by many to Mosby for his earlier use of it in an 1876 newspaper article. The long article by Mosby was actually a reprinted letter to a former Confederate who had asked Mosby to support Samuel Tilden, the Democratic presidential nominee. In his response Mosby went to great lengths to explain why he was supporting Rutherford Hayes, the Republican.[7] Mosby believed that the Southern people would be better served without the political solidarity they were showing for the Democrats. "The sectional unity of the Southern people has been the governing idea and bane of their politics. So long as it continues the war will be a controlling element of politics; for any cry in the South that unifies the Confederates re-echoes through the North and rekindles the war fires there."[8]

1. Reader's Digest Assoc., *Family Encyclopedia*, 233.
2. The *Belgic* sailed under the White Star/Occidental SS Company flag in joint service between San Francisco, Yokohama, and Hong Kong. "House Flags of U.S. Shipping Companies," http://flagspot.net/flags/us.
3. *New York Herald*, August 12, 1876.
4. Ramage, *Gray Ghost*, 218–19; Mosby's son Beverly was living in Ogden, Utah, and his other son, John, was in Denver. Captain Dolly is Major Dolly. It is unknown why Mosby used the lesser rank in this letter.
5. *Richmond Dispatch*, September 16, 1894; this article by Mosby largely dealt with some of his more interesting scouts for Gen. Jeb Stuart in 1862–1863.
6. John T. Kincheloe Collection.
7. Reader's Digest Assoc., *Family Encyclopedia*, 501, 502. In a disputed election, Tilden won the popular vote; Hayes became president as a result of "backroom" maneuvering known as The Comprise of 1877.
8. *New York Herald*, August 12, 1876.

Shaving Sheridan with a Sharp Razor

Colonel Mosby extracted some measure of reciprocation from General Sheridan through his writings in various periodicals.

Nov. 28th/94   San Francisco
Captain S. F. Chapman

Dear Sam—

Rec'd your letter—I leave here for the East Saturday—as I stop at several places can't tell you when I shall get to

Covington.[1] Of course I wd. prefer to reach there in the daytime or early in the night as I have a horror of being waked up at night. So write me all about the trains to Louisville (c/o Major Dolly, 1231 4th Avenue). I expect to get there about the 8th or 9th of December. Munson[2] lives in St. Louis & I have promised to stop over with him. I expect Dolly will buy up the whole edition of *Harper's Weekly* when the Blazer piece appears. Hope it will come out before I get there as I want to see him with his feathers on. I have finished my Sheridan article & sent it off to Stuart[3]—don't know when or where it will be published. I did not go for Phil after Rosser's[4] style, with a tomahawk & butcher knife, but shaved him with a sharp razor. I had no idea what a brute he was until I read his telegrams—all of wch. he suppresses in his memoirs. It is more aggressive than anything I have heretofore written. I am no longer a defendant—having the record to stand on I become an assailant & show that Sheridan was accusing us of doing what he was all the time doing. Got a letter from Colonel Chapman yesterday. I wrote him that I wd. like for him to come to Washington while I am there—Got an offer to lecture in Louisville for a Presbyterian Church—declined, as I never believed in infant damnation. You know a few years ago the Presbyterians were talking about changing their creed on this point. I asked Bill Williamson[5] at Warrenton if it wd. be retroactive & release the souls of all the babies in Hell that they had damned—he said it wd. I got an invitation yesterday from a lecture board in Washington to deliver a series of lectures—declined. I am sorry that I shall not be here when Willie returns. Love to your wife.

Sincerely yours,
Jno. S. Mosby[6]

Although married to a devout Catholic, Mosby declined religious affiliation, stating at one point in a letter, while speaking of his friend Joe Bryan, "He [Joe] is a Christian, I am not."[7] Mosby often made challenging comments about religion such as the ones here about the Presbyterians. He was probably best described as being agnostic. Rosser was a West Point classmate and friend of George A. Custer but not of Gen. Philip Sheridan, Custer's superior. Colonel Mosby was a life-long antagonist of both Custer and Sheridan, always believing Custer responsible for the brutal execution of six of Sam Chapman's men at Front Royal in 1864. Two months later Mosby retaliated against a like number of Custer's men whom he had captured. Years later Custer told his old friend Rosser that he was not responsible for the executions—Mosby never believed it.[8]

1. Covington, Virginia, Sam Chapman's home.
2. Maj. John Munson, who served in Mosby's command, authored *Reminiscences of a Mosby Guerrilla* in 1906.
3. Virginia Stuart (Mosby) Coleman, Colonel Mosby's daughter.
4. Faust, *Encyclopedia of the Civil War*; Thomas L. Rosser was a Confederate general who commanded the famous Laurel Brigade. He was an intimate friend and West Point classmate of Gen. George Custer.
5. Not known but Williamson was probably a local Presbyterian minister.
6. John T. Kincheloe Collection.
7. Mitchell, *The Letters of John S. Mosby,* 2nd ed., 103, John Mosby to Bob Walker, June 30, 1900.
8. Mitchell, *The Letters of John S. Mosby,* 97–98; John Mosby to Bob Walker, December 12, 1899.

"He Is a Noble Boy"

Colonel Mosby continued in his admiration of Sam's son Willie and asked for Sam's remembrances of the war.

—————

April 10th, 1895   Southern Pacific Company
Captain S. F. Chapman   Law Department
                                            San Francisco

Dear Sam—
    Willie sailed for Hong Kong at midnight on the 4th. He came to see me every evening while he was here. He is a noble boy & you ought to be very proud of him. He brought me from Japan a tortoise shell paper cutter—It so happened the first use I made of it was to open a letter from you. Within the next four months I want you to furnish me with your historical

memoranda. The *N.Y. World*[1] on Sunday, March 31st has an article I wrote in wch. I allude to you. I was careful to speak oftener of William than of you. Love to your family. Kind regards to my cousins.

Very truly,
Jno. S. Mosby[2]

Colonel Mosby's article in the New York paper related his attack on a large Federal wagon train carrying provisions and arms to General Sheridan's army in the Shenandoah Valley. The attack resulted in the capture of large numbers of men and wagons and the destroying of a huge amount of supplies. The article mentioned Sam and William Chapman as leaders in the attack. However, in Mosby's memoirs and at least one interview he says that "The gallant Capt. Sam Chapman, commanding Company E, although burning for the strife, was prudently held in reserve."[3] The reference to William was to Sam's younger brother who became Mosby's second-in-command during the war. In 1864 William Chapman married Josie Jeffries, a young lady from a well-established family of Fauquier County, Virginia. Mosby often hinted of his disdain for both Josie and her mother in his postwar letters to Sam. They were evidently, in Mosby's view, the domineering members of William's family.

1. *New York World*, March 31, 1895.
2. Stuart-Mosby Historical Society Collection.
3. *New York World*, March 31, 1895; Mewborn, "*From Mosby's Command*," 148; U.S. War Department, *War of the Rebellion: Official Records*, 43:1, 634; Brown, *Mosby's Fighting Parson*, 302.

Losing Souls If He Leaves

While Colonel Mosby planned another trip east from San Francisco he spoke of Col. William Chapman being away from his mother-in-law and of former Ranger Syd Ferguson not attending the command's first reunion in Alexandria the previous winter.

Aug. 18th [1895]   930 Bush St., S.F.
Captain S. F. Chapman

Dear Sam—

Willie arrived yesterday from Hong Kong looking as well
& handsome as ever. I shall start East next month—will stop
to see a cousin of mine at Huntington & also to see you, &
John Munson in St. Louis. Should think William wd. be very
glad there is a long distance between him & his mother-in-
law. Yesterday I recd. from *Harper's Weekly* the proofs of my
Blazer article. They were corrected & immediately returned;
presume will appear next week. I have certainly done full
justice to Major Dolly. I take just as much pride in what the
command did when I wasn't present in a fight as if I had been
there. I think the Rev. Sid [*sic*] might have left the mourners
one night to attend the reunion. I never could see the sense
of people mourning at the prospect of going to Heaven. You
know Sid wrote he couldn't come up from Fredericksburg last
winter for fear that several souls wd. be lost if he left. Love to
your family.

John S. Mosby (over)[1]

I suspect that Sid could send (& has sent) more people to
Heaven by shooting at them than by preaching. Read your
letter to Willie—that fighting boy of yours is evidently a son of
his father.

———————

In the Blazer fight Colonel Mosby was not present and Dolly Richards
was in command. Blazer's force was soundly defeated. Ranger Sydnor
Ferguson[2] captured Captain Blazer by running him down, while both
were on horseback, and hitting him with his revolver.[3] This is the same
fight often referred to in other letters from Mosby in which Tom Richards, Dolly's brother, felt he was not given due recognition or "justice"
for his part in the fight and that Dolly received all the accolades. Notice that Mosby did not miss an opportunity to make a disparaging
reference to William Chapman's mother-in-law.

1. John T. Kincheloe Collection.
2. Snydor "Syd" Gilbert Ferguson. Mosby used "Sid" in his letters. Ferguson became a minister after the war.
3. Munson, *Reminiscences*, 121.

"If Jessie James Were Living"

Colonel Mosby continued to take a very personal—even paternal—approach to Sam's son Willie. The same could not be said of his approach to Mrs. Jeffries, Sam's brother's mother-in-law. And Mosby continued to have ardent feelings concerning things political—this time in the debate over the free coinage of silver as opposed to the country's adoption of a gold standard.

July 25th [1897]   930 Bush St.
Captain S. F. Chapman   S.F.

Dear Sam—
    I have just read the enclosed from Willie. You see that he is improving his mind as well as filling his purse. He is fond of reading & I encourage him in it. In this way he will prepare himself for something better. There are a good many books on the steamer—most of wch. he has read. This voyage I gave him several to read, among them *The Memoirs of S. S. Prentiss,* who I regard as one of the most lovable & wonderful men that ever lived.[1] William writes me that he has been transferred to St. Louis. Munson knows a great many nice people there—I had a splendid time there last winter, shall stop there again on my way east in September when I hope also to see you. Did you see my last article in *Once a Week?* I have been feeling a great deal of anxiety about Fount—he has been sick with Typhoid Fever but is now recovering.[2] I don't suppose William will take old Mrs. Jeffries to St. Louis.[3] If Jesse James were living he might relieve William of any future care over her. Haven't heard from Major Dolly for a long time—never hear from Tom.[4] I sent you two of Carlisle's[5] speeches on the silver question. You know that I have always been opposed

to the full coinage of silver. It is simply a new phase of the old greenback currency. If you had one barrel of sugar & were to put enough sand in it to have two barrels, would you have any more sugar? You can't make people richer by debasing the currency. If the people want cheap money give them old Confederate notes. If the mere fiat of Government can create money why not make it out of iron & declare that a pound of gold shall be equal to a pound of iron after the iron is coined. Cleveland[6] has certainly done two good things—he has sat down the silver craze & he has broken up the Republican Party. I would not be surprised if Kentucky goes Republican this fall. Willie is due here about August 14th. I have all three of my boys (Willie-Clay-Ernest) at work now.[7] Love to your family.

Sincerely,

Jno. S. Mosby[8]

---

1. Sergeant Smith Prentiss was the "silver-tongued orator" from the nineteenth century, a leader of the Whig political party, a congressman, and lawyer.

2. Brown, *Mosby's Fighting Parson*, 192–93; Keen and Mewborn, *43rd Battalion*, 295 (roster); Fountain "Fount" Beattie, one of the original nine men with Mosby who preceded the formation of the Forty-third Battalion known as Mosby's Rangers. Beattie became Sam Chapman's choice for lieutenant when E Company, commanded by Sam, was formed in 1864.

3. Col. William Chapman's mother-in-law.

4. Maj. A. E. "Dolly" Richards and his brother Capt. Tom Richards.

5. John Griffin Carlisle, secretary of the treasury during President Cleveland's administration (1893–1897), was a strong advocate of the gold standard during the "free silver" debate.

6. President Grover Cleveland.

7. Willie Chapman, son of Sam; Clay and Ernest Beattie, sons of Fount. The three young men had gone west "seeking their fortunes" with an assist from John Mosby, who would remark, "I am very proud of my three protégés" (GLC 3921.13. 20 January 1906, The Gilder Lehrman Collection, courtesy of The Gilder Lehrman Institute of American History, New York).

8. GLC 3921.01. John Mosby. Autograph letter signed: to Sam Chapman, 25 July [1897] (The Gilder Lehrman Collection, courtesy of The Gilder Lehrman Institute of American History, New York).

Choosing between Free Silver

Colonel Mosby was a resident of California for some twelve years, and prior to that was in Hong Kong for nearly seven. His prosaic position with the railroad was like sand in his shoes and he itched for a return to the familiar environs of Washington, D.C., and northern Virginia. Additionally, he had suffered a terrible accident when he was struck in the head by a skittish horse during a trip back east earlier in the year. His fractured skull was healing but he lost an eye to the surgeon's knife, which made him all the more despondent returning to a livelihood that he had no desire to resume.

Sept. 22nd/97   781 Sutter St., S.F.

Dear Sam:

Herewith my check for $20 on account of Willie—He brought over a Canton cape for me on his last trip. I don't know what it cost—he did not send me any bill but I presume you need more, so I pay this now & will settle with Willie when he returns. I have been expecting to hear about the Covington P.O. after your interview with McKinley.[1] I haven't the slightest expectation of getting anything. Some of my friends thought he had reserved the Guatemala mission for me as it was one of the places wch. I indicated to him. I did not agree with him on his not having appointed a single Confederate to any foreign place—showed it was design not accident. Today I see that he has promised Guatemala to Hunter of Ky.[2] It is hard to have to choose between free silver & Mark Hanna.[3] Brady[4] wrote me that he was going to see McKinley last week.

I still hope you may come out all right.

Very truly yours—Jno. S. Mosby[5]

While trying to land a post for himself in the government, Colonel Mosby was also doing what he could to find something for Sam Chapman. A postmaster's appointment in Sam's hometown of Covington,

Virginia, was promising and friends had managed to secure for him a sitting with the president. However, the position went to Howard Revercomb, a member of a wellborn Republican family. The irony was that Howard was a brother to Sam's son-in-law, George Revercomb.[6] Mosby was torn between remaining loyal to his Republican leanings and President McKinley and supporting the alternative, the populist "free silver" faction, which he typically railed against. Yet remaining loyal to McKinley meant supporting the president's biggest player, Mark Hanna. While visiting friends at the University of Virginia in Charlottesville, Mosby was kicked in the face and head by a horse. The resultant fractured skull put him in a critical state, with his doctors placing his chances of rapid recovery at 50 percent. However, he surprised them all, including the doctors and by mid-August was back in San Francisco.[7]

1. President William McKinley (1896–1904).

2. *Biographical Directory of the United States Congress;* Hunter, a native of Belfast, Ireland, was previously a Republican congressman from Kentucky. He served as minister to Guatemala and Honduras from 1897 to 1902, and returned to Congress in 1903.

3. Reader's Digest Assoc., *Family Encyclopedia,* 490–91; a soon-to-be senator from Ohio, Hanna was a wealthy businessman who engineered McKinley's two presidential campaigns.

4. *Biographical Directory; Richmond Dispatch,* September 2, 1897; James D. Brady, former Republican congressman, was the newly appointed chief collector of Internal Revenue.

5. GLC 3921.02. John Mosby. Autograph letter signed: to Sam Chapman, 22 September 1897 (The Gilder Lehrman Collection, courtesy of The Gilder Lehrman Institute of American History, New York).

6. Brown, *Mosby's Fighting Parson,* 323; Sam Chapman's daughter Lizzie was married to George Revercomb.

7. *San Francisco Call,* April 28, 1897; Siepel, *Rebel,* 250–51.

"He Is Eminently Worthy"

Sam Chapman, unable to secure placement with the government, grew weary of his never-ending pastoral responsibilities. He set his hopes on something very familiar—a return to the battlefield. Almost thirty-three years to the day when he laid down his arms and took the loyalty oath to the United States, he was ready to don the blue uniform that he fought so valiantly against. The country had entered into war with Spain over Cuba. Sam's age, and possibly his then-ordained profession, kept him off the front lines, but each regiment going into battle had the complement of one commissioned chaplain.

———❦———

June 9, 1898   United States Senate
Col. Pettit 4th U.S. Vols.   Washington, D.C.
War Dept.

Dear Sir:

This will present Rev. Samuel F. Chapman who we ask may be named as chaplain of your regiment, in accordance with your kind proffer.

He is eminently worthy.

Jno. S. Mosby
Jno. W. Daniel
Thomas S. Martin
Covington, Va.[1]

———❦———

The above request, written in John Mosby's hand and signed by him and the two Virginia senators, secured for Sam Chapman a commission as chaplain and a trip to Cuba.[2] Ironically, while aiding Chapman in securing a wartime position in the military, Mosby was unable to obtain one for himself. When he volunteered his services in the spring of 1898, the following telegrams were exchanged between Mosby and Gen. Nelson A. Miles, commander in chief of the U.S. Army: "I would be very glad to have your services but think it will require some influence. Suggest that you communicate with your Senators" (Miles to Mosby, May 4, 1898). "Your telegram received. I have no influence except my military record" (Mosby to Miles, May 4, 1898). The newspapers of the day, from California to Washington, D.C., milked the story for all its worth. According to the *San Francisco Call*, the person behind Mosby's inability to obtain a place to serve was none other than Secretary of War Russell A. Alger, an old nemesis from the Civil War. Mosby gave credence to this in a letter to the *Richmond Times*, saying, "The criticisms of General Miles do him a great injustice. . . .

[He] is not the appointing power."³ The following year Mosby raised a cavalry troop, Mosby's Hussars, but their greatest achievement would be not a victory over the Spanish in Cuba but serving as hosts for a July Fourth concert and ball at which the invited guests included the governor of California and San Francisco's mayor.⁴

1. John T. Kincheloe Collection.
2. Brown, *Mosby's Fighting Parson*, 327.
3. *Richmond Times*, November 12, 1899; Alger was a colonel with the Fifth Michigan, under the command of George Custer, when Mosby's men executed several of the Michigan soldiers who had been captured. This was in retaliation for the shooting and hanging of some of the captured partisans, under the command of Capt. Sam Chapman.
4. *San Francisco Call*, May 6, 1898; May 11, 1898; May 13, 1898; June 24, 1898; July 4, 1898.

"My Retaliation Was a Merciful Act"

In September 1864, while Mosby was recovering from a wound, Capt. Sam Chapman led a detachment of the Rangers in an attack on a Union Army wagon train just south of Front Royal, Virginia. In the ensuing fight six of Chapman's men were captured; later that same day they were brutally executed. When Mosby returned to duty, he took retaliation by ordering the execution of a like number of Union prisoners. In this letter Mosby finally revealed the facts behind his retaliatory action.

———————

August 26th / 99   705 Post St., S.F.

Dear Sam—

Yesterday I mailed to Joe Bryan¹ an article wch. for the first time will give to the world a true account of the Front Royal affair.² The world has never known that I reported it to Genl. Lee & that both he & Secretary Seddon³ not only approved but ordered me to do it. I don't remember whether or not I recd. their order before actually doing it. I rather infer from the dates that I had not recd. it. You will see that my letter to Genl. Lee does not ask for instructions—it tells him what I was going to do & I did it. I always kept it a secret that I had the order. I did not want to shirk responsibility for doing what I thought was right. The publication of the war records began when I was in Hong Kong.[4] When I went to Washington, Genl. Marcus Wright[5] asked me to let them have all my official papers to copy—wch. I did. Among them is my original letter to Genl. Lee with endorsements. I have it now—Scott's book was published in 1867[6]—we were then under military rule. Genl. Lee & Seddon were living. It makes no allusion to their instructions. I never did anything that my conscience more thoroughly approved—that Torbert-Merritt-& Custer[7] were ashamed of hanging my men is proved by their not alluding to it in their reports. My retaliation was a merciful act. It saved the lives of both our men & the Yankees. The war wd. have degenerated into a massacre. You may remember that old Lowell made his private secretary telegraph a Boston newspaper as a reproach to Grant that he had put you in the P.O. Dept.—red handed with the blood of Union soldiers killed at the house burnings near Berryville.[8]—that I took the responsibility made the Wash. Correspondent telegraph his paper that Mosby said the men killed were house burners & that if he was ever caught at such work in Boston he wd. expect to be treated in the same way. I also informed Grant about it—he dismissed both old Lowell & his Secretary. There are no more Grants. When I was in Hong Kong Sam Bagby through Ned Burke preferred the same charges against Col. Chapman. He was called on to answer it. He got from Genl. Sewell, his Chief, time allowed before answering, to write me & get a reply. He wrote me of the accusations against him for obeying my orders. I promptly replied I assumed all the responsibility for the act—said that I ordered all men caught house burning to be shot on the spot & that if anyone should be punished & dismissed from office that I was the guilty man. He wrote me that he put in his defense that my letter was satisfactory. As you were in command I hope that you will be at the unveiling of the monument. Take this letter with you & show it to

the men & give them all my love. My kind regards to your
family.

Yours Sincerely,

Jno. S. Mosby[9]

⟶▸◂⟵

At the time Mosby sent this letter to Sam Chapman he sent a similar
article to former Ranger Joe Bryan's newspaper, the *Richmond Times*.[10]
The reference to Grant having "put you in the P.O. Dept.—red-handed
with the blood of Union soldiers" was a reference to Sam Chapman's
appointment, as well as his brother William's, to the Railway Postal
Service during President Grant's administration. Sam and William led
the Rangers in the attack on the house burners near Berryville in August 1864, in which the order was given that no prisoners were to be
taken. Colonel Mosby asked Sam to take the letter to Front Royal the
following month when a monument to the executed Confederates was
dedicated.

    1. A former Ranger with Mosby, owner and publisher of the *Richmond
Times*.
    2. Brown, *Mosby's Fighting Parson*, 225–34, 252–55.
    3. Confederate secretary of war (1862–1865).
    4. U.S. War Department, *War of the Rebellion: A Compilation of
the Official Records of the Union and Confederate Armies (128 volumes,
1881–1901)*.
    5. Former Confederate who served the United States as primary agent
for the collection of Confederate archives. His work became an integral part
of the *Official Records*.
    6. Scott, *Partisan Life with Col. John S. Mosby*.
    7. Generals Alfred Torbert, Wesley Merritt, and George Custer, all three
Union field commanders during the Front Royal executions.
    8. *Richmond Times*, November 10, 1899; Brown, *Mosby's Fighting Par-
son*, 212–14; on August 20, 1864, elements of General Custer's Fifth Michigan Cavalry were in the process of burning homes of private citizens near
Berryville, Virginia, when they were attacked by Mosby's men under the command of Col. William Chapman and Capt. Sam Chapman. No prisoners were
taken by the Southerners.
    9. John T. Kincheloe Collection.
    10. November 10, 1899.

"As If He Were My Own Son"

Colonel Mosby saw Tom Richards again and found him still bitter over his alleged treatment by his younger brother, Dolly. Although Tom was the older of the two by fifteen years, he was always subordinate to Dolly in rank. Tom's actions in the Blazer fight probably led to the overwhelming victory by the Rangers. But Tom complained on several occasions of the "injustice" he received from Dolly regarding the events.

————

[Second page of an 1899 letter with first page missing. Exact date and location unknown but probably San Francisco, where Mosby was a lawyer.]

I was in San Francisco last week—saw Tom Richards—he has lost every cent he had in booms & speculation.[1] Tom complained to me that Dolly did him injustices about the Blazer fight. I was rather vexed about it. Dolly never made any written report of it. I always understood & have so stated that he ordered Co. B to charge without orders—he always got the credit.[2] Of course in a certain sense a commander gets the credit of what his subordinates do. But he also gets the blame of failure. Willie is due here on the 27th—always comes straight to my room as soon as he lands. I feel toward him as if he were my son—everybody falls in love with him. Love to your family.

Sincerely,
Jno. S. Mosby[3]

I have recd. a letter from Fitz Lee saying he was about to publish a life of Genl. Lee[4] & asking me to get him a good agent, which I did. I was rather surprised at his writing to me—he never was my friend—tried to prevent my having a command.

————

Mosby had reason to be surprised at Fitz Lee's request. Their dislike for each other went back to the days of John Mosby's service in the

First Virginia Cavalry at the beginning of the war. After General Stuart gave Mosby fifteen men from the First Virginia commanded by Fitz Lee to begin his own command, Fitz Lee demanded that Mosby return the men to the First Virginia. General Stuart overruled the order.[5]

1. Keen and Mewborn, *43rd Battalion*, 361 (roster); Tom Richards was a real estate broker in Los Angeles when Mosby saw him on this occasion.
2. Ibid., 220; Siepel, *Rebel*, 131; Tom Richards's sudden attack, leading Company B upon the Blazer Scouts, although without orders from his brother, Dolly, who was in command, was both the beginning and the ending of the vicious fight. It was so sudden and violent that the Union cavalrymen could not recover.
3. Horace Mewborn Collection.
4. Fitzhugh Lee, *General Lee*, 1899.
5. Mosby, *The Memoirs of Colonel John S. Mosby*, 184–85.

"Phil Was a Great Liar"

The following is a portion of a letter from Colonel Mosby to Sam Chapman's son Willie, who lived in San Francisco but was visiting at his father's home in Covington, Virginia. It is included here for the remarks Mosby made regarding Generals Custer and Sheridan and Maj. Dolly Richards, concerning the executions at Front Royal, Virginia, of six Rangers by Union cavalrymen. Note the contumelious affronts to William Chapman's wife and mother-in-law. Much of the letter, however, is illegible.

———

Nov. 1st 99   705 Post St.
                                                 S.F.

Dear Willie:

I recd. Your letter today & was glad to get it. I was a little uneasy about your returning. Matt Fletcher told me that you spoke of going into business in Covington. I hope you will be here long enough for us to go around a little. [Much of this part of the letter is illegible]

Yesterday I sent Joe Bryan a reply to Richards' address in

reference to Gen. Grant.[1] I had to steer between two rocky shores to defend Grant without wounding Dolly & my own men. It was like crossing Niagara on a rope. I think I put a new face on the matter without compromising myself. What Richards said was true but he did not say the whole truth. I think Sam will laugh at my defense of Phil Sheridan.[2] The truth is the records prove that Phil was a great liar or, according to his own statement, a murderer. I give him the benefit of the doubt & so he was a great liar. My article will appear in the *Times* Sunday, Nov. 12th, so you can read it before you return.[3] Dolly thought he had discovered a wasp's nest when he said Custer had nothing to do with the hangings. Col. Peters[4] wrote me that Dolly's allusion to Gen. Grant uncalled for & in bad taste considering my relations with Grant. Ask Sam if he doesn't think that when Grant telegraphed Sheridan about capturing and corralling my men's wives it would have been a great advantage & promoted the efficiency of my command if he had done it, i.e., Josie & Mrs. Jeffries.[5] Grant's order included mothers-in-law as well as wives. I have no doubt it would have been a great favor to many of my men if Sheridan had executed the order.[6] I have been expecting a letter from Sam about the unveiling. I want the Republicans to carry Kentucky & the Democrats Ohio. That would give Mark Hanna & the Philippines a black eye. All my love to your father & mother.

Very truly
Jno. S. Mosby[7]

Willie Chapman did return to the West Coast but not before setting up a cash store business in Covington for his brothers to run. It would be some twenty years more before Willie returned to Covington for good.[8] The speech that Dolly Richards gave, at the dedication of the monument in Front Royal, relieved Custer of responsibility for the executions and placed it squarely on the shoulders of Generals Grant and Sheridan. Mosby strongly disagreed and took great umbrage over Dolly's remarks about his friend General Grant. Grant did issue an order to Sheridan in August 1864 that read in part: "The families of most of Mosby's men are known and can be collected. I think they should be taken . . . and kept . . . as hostages for the good conduct of Mosby and his men."[9] In his response to Dolly Richards's remarks that Grant was responsible for the executions, Mosby exposed General Sheridan for making false reports to Grant on his—Sheridan's—activities in the Shenandoah Valley against Colonel Mosby, and prior to the executions of the Confederates. Sheridan attested to having hanged several of Mosby's men for "annoying him" and made light of the deeds of Mosby's men against him. Speaking of the Berryville wagon raid of August 13, 1864, Sheridan said, "Mosby has annoyed me and captured a few wagons (6)."[10] Actually, Mosby and his men captured and destroyed seventy-five loaded wagons and took over two hundred prisoners. Sheridan told Grant that he had hanged and shot several of the partisan's men and captured three hundred prisoners—all Mosby's men. These stories were fabricated and/or embellished according to official records. However, Mosby did not accuse Sheridan of the responsibility for the executions at Front Royal, as Sheridan was not present; he placed blame primarily on General Custer and explained why he held these views.

1. *Richmond Times,* November 12, 1899. On September 23, 1899, the thirty-fifth anniversary of the Front Royal executions, a monument was dedicated and Maj. Dolly Richards gave the keynote address. Richards absolved General Custer of any blame and placed the blame for the brutal killings squarely on the shoulders of Generals Sheridan and Grant.
2. Sam Chapman was aware of Mosby's strong feelings toward Sheridan so Mosby thought Sam might be surprised when reading of his defense of Sheridan in this instance.
3. Mosby's reply: "I acquit Sheridan of all responsibility for the deed at Front Royal."
4. Haselberger, *Confederate Retaliation,* 95–96. Col. William E. Peters commanded the Twenty-first Virginia Cavalry and was placed under arrest for refusing an order to burn the town of Chambersburg, Pennsylvania, in 1864.
5. Josie Jeffries, wife of William Chapman, and Mrs. Jeffries, his mother-in-law.
6. *Richmond Times,* November 12, 1899; in response to reports General Grant was receiving from General Sheridan, relative to Mosby and his men, Grant was probably under the impression "that these Children of the Mist lived in a territory a few miles square." This quotation is contained in the letter to the newspaper in response to Dolly Richards's address at Front Royal.

"Children of the Mist" apparently referred to Mosby's men who seemed to vanish after a raid. Authority and/or prior usage unknown.

7. GLC 3921.03. John Mosby. Autograph letter signed: to Wm. A. Chapman, 1 November 1899 (The Gilder Lehrman Collection, courtesy of The Gilder Lehrman Institute of American History, New York).

8. Brown, *Mosby's Fighting Parson,* 334.

9. Ibid., 208; U.S. War Department, *War of the Rebellion* 43:1, 811.

10. *Richmond Times,* November 12, 1899.

"As Young as I Was at the Miskel Gate"

Colonel Mosby was back in California with the railroad, very unhappy, and still longing for another position and location, preferably in the service of the United States government. He felt bitter over President McKinley's failure to appoint him to a position after his loyal support for him in the 1896 election.[1] But regardless of his feelings he again voted for McKinley in the fall election. And he remained committed in his efforts of finding a place for his longtime confidant Sam Chapman. The patronage-heavy, scandal-ridden postal service appeared to be the best bet. (Santa Cruz is south of San Francisco on Monterey Bay.)

June 4, 1900   Santa Cruz Powder Works
                                                Santa Cruz, Cal.

Dear Sam:

I came down here yesterday to enjoy an outing by the sea. Mr. Robertson—whom I had never seen but who is an enthusiastic friend of Willie's, as well as of all your family—[illegible] his wife & mother-in-law, Mrs. Miller [illegible] with him—drove into town (having heard that I was coming) & brought me out to their home wch. is situated in a lovely canyon.[2] Here in the fresh air I feel like a new man. I am so much refreshed that I shall stay until tomorrow afternoon—besides I have promised to come often & bring Willie with me when he returns from his next trip from Hong Kong about 15th of July. A year ago I gave him a pass to visit the Robertsons—for some reason he did not come. The place is a perfect Eden (no serpent). I just wish you could be here with me. I wd. feel as young as I was at Miskel's gate when I burst out laughing in the midst of the fight when I saw you standing in your stirrups whaling the Yankees with your sabre.[3] They all admire Mrs. Chapman as much as they do you. Well, I wrote to you about your applying for a place in the postal service in "the provinces." Late disclosure show that integrity, as well as experience, is needed in it. I have written to John Daniel[4] & asked him to help you. I am sure you can get a place if you will only rouse yourself & try (Take a few lessons in that sort of tact & skill from Colonel William & Josie.)[5] If you will get in now it will in all probability be a life appointment. I do not expect to go East before December. I have a horror of being in Va. during a presidential election.[6] [Remainder of letter is missing].[7]

Sam's brother William had a good position with the Internal Revenue Service. Sam Chapman may not have been in the best frame of mind for job hunting at that particular time. Less than four weeks earlier, from the date of Mosby's letter, Sam's twenty-five-year-old son, Elgin, drowned in Jackson River, which flowed behind Covington Baptist Church. Although not documented, it is the belief by many that his death was a suicide. Added to this was the fact that Sam's wife, Rebecca, was seriously ill.[8]

1. Siepel, *Rebel*, 255.

2. Further identities of the Robertson family and Mrs. Miller are not known but apparently they were friends of Willie Chapman and his father.

3. Mosby, *Mosby's War Reminiscences*, 108–9. In the Miskel Farm fight of April 1, 1863, Sam Chapman had emptied his revolvers and was swinging his saber at his enemies while standing up in his stirrups. The scene was later drawn for *Leslie's Illustrated Newspaper* by the artist James E. Taylor, based on a description given by Mosby, and published in former Ranger James Williamson's book, *Mosby's Rangers*, in 1896.

4. Daniel was a U.S. senator from Virginia, a former Confederate officer, and friend to both Mosby and Chapman.

5. Col. William Chapman and his wife.

6. Siepel, *Rebel*, xvii (introduction). On a past occasion Mosby was asked

if he believed in Hell: "Of course. Any Southerner who did not obviously had never tried to vote Republican and live in Virginia," he replied.

7. Horace Mewborn Collection.

8. Brown, *Mosby's Fighting Parson*, 334–35.

"As You Have Little to Do"

The election was over and McKinley was back in the White House. Mosby asked Senator Daniel to remember Sam Chapman in case another chaplain's commission became available in the Army.

Nov. 23rd, 1900   705 Post St.
                                                   S. F.

Dear Sam:

Although you are in my debt for several letters I drop you a line to tell you that I have just got a letter from him [Daniel] in wch. he says—"I will certainly remember Capt. Sam Chapman for I feel an interest in him & will be glad to serve him & will do so to the extent of my power." I had asked him to look out for you if the Army is reorganized this winter. I spent two days last week with the Robertsons. I think as you have little to do you might write me oftener than you [do]. My love to your family. My regards to Dr. Wm. Rogers. Have you heard how Josie voted?

                                                   Yours truly,
                                                   Jno. S. Mosby[1]

Daniel says in his letter—"I am going on my own hook someday to find out McKinley's true inwardness toward you. I am not satisfied about it."

Colonel Mosby, in chastising Sam for not writing, may not have been aware of the seriousness of Sam's wife's illness. She was stricken with Bright's disease and died just over one week from the date of Mosby's letter. She was fifty-six years old.[2] Mosby's failure to mention it—he closed with only "my love to your family"—would indicate this. His question on Josie's voting belies what he was really asking: how did William Chapman vote? Women were still disenfranchised.

1. GLC 3921.04. John Mosby. Autograph letter signed: to Sam Chapman, 23 November 1900 (The Gilder Lehrman Collection, courtesy of The Gilder Lehrman Institute of American History, New York).
2. Brown, *Mosby's Fighting Parson*, 335.

"I Have No Political Influence"

In February 1901 Colonel Mosby lost his position with the Southern Pacific Railroad. Its founder and owner, C. P. Huntington, was an old friend from the days of President Grant, and as long as he was in charge Mosby was secure. However, Huntington died in 1900, spelling the end of the Colonel's sixteen years with the company.[1] Then sixty-seven years old and jobless, Mosby was forced once again to cash in any favors he still had in his political bank. This time McKinley came through and Mosby found himself an agent in the Department of Interior's Land Management Office—not exactly what he had hoped for, but it was a job, and that is what he desperately needed.

July 25th 1901   Alexandria

Dear Sam:

Just recd. your letter. I wrote to you yesterday enclosing one from John Daniel. If he will go with you to see Root or Hitchcock he can get you appointed in the Philippines or Supervisor of Forests. I wanted you to stay in March & get something. I have no political influence. It was an accident I got what I have but I shall not hold it long. It is no use for you to come to Washington without Daniel.

I leave in a few days.

Yours truly, Jno. S. Mosby[2]

Mosby had given Sam the only advice he could then—to use what friendship he had with Senator Daniel, come to Washington, and have him to accompany him to see Elihu Root, the secretary of war, or Ethan Allen Hitchcock, the secretary of the interior. The U.S. Army was in the midst of change since Root became secretary in 1899, and the insurgency in the Philippines was still raging—raising the possibility of a chaplain's commission for the sixty-three-year-old Cuba veteran. Or Hitchcock may have been able to use Chapman in his forestry service.

1. Siepel, *Rebel*, 246, 256.
2. GLC 3921.05. John Mosby. Autograph letter signed: to Sam Chapman, 25 July 1901 (The Gilder Lehrman Collection, courtesy of The Gilder Lehrman Institute of American History, New York).

Mosby Chastises His Old Friend

Sam Chapman apparently did not take Mosby's advice to meet in person Senator Daniel and have Daniel go with him to see prospective heads of departments to whom Sam could apply for a position.

———

Aug. 1st 1901   Washington, D.C.

Dear Sam:

I have your letter with enclosure. I cannot see that you have any just ground to complain against John Daniel—on the contrary, I think he has been very kind to you. He was certainly at the Inauguration—also at the extra session a few days afterward, for I dined with him at his house. He may have gone to Va. for a few days. He was at his house here all the time for the last two months afterward. His Secretary was there all the time. If you had you could have seen him nearly every day. It seems that he endorsed your application & forwarded it & got the reply of "no vacancy." But that is the stereotyped answer to all applications by mail. I told you there would be no use in applying in that way, you must go in person with Daniel. Of course I did not expect Daniel to quit his seat in the Convention to come here to get a place for you. But he will be here next Winter. I have no political influence. If I had you would get the benefit of it. Daniel has not certainly shown an indisposition to help you. You seem to forget that he had you sent as a Chaplain into Cuba. He was not to blame for not being at home when you called there last March. You might have waited for his return. Neither is it Daniel's fault that Hitchcock says there are "no vacancies." Daniel did all you asked him to do.

Very truly,

Jno. S. Mosby[1]

1. GLC 3921.06. John Mosby. Autograph letter signed: to Sam Chapman, 1 August 1901 (The Gilder Lehrman Collection, courtesy of The Gilder Lehrman Institute of American History, New York).

"Is Josie for Roosevelt or Parker?"

After nearly three years in the Department of the Interior's Land Management Office Mosby had, at last, gotten a position with the Department of Justice in Washington. And he was still very much in the political arena, working for the election of Republicans in the forthcoming congressional races. He was very confident of the favorable outcome in certain Virginia districts as well as of Roosevelt's return to the presidency for a full four-year term, following his three-year term due to McKinley's assassination.

Sept. 10th 1904   Department of Justice
                                   Washington

Dear Sam:

I have just recd. a letter from Brown Allen[1] with a copy of the *Old Dominion Sun* with my letter.[2] I am very anxious for Revercomb to be elected.[3] A quiet-still hunt is the best for him. Is the National Committee helping him? Agnew[4] told me they had given Slemp $2500.[5] The Democrats are all indifferent. I have not seen one who thinks that Parker has any chance. I have asked Agnew—Willie—& Brown Allen to get Tom Watson to speak in Revercomb's, Slemp's, & Hoge's[6] districts.

If he will I think they will be all three elected. On Monday the *Wash. Post* will publish a letter from me signed J. S. M. I want Revercomb to read it. I would like to hear from you. Is Josie for Roosevelt or Parker? I sent Colonel William a paper with my letter. He took no notice of it.

Yours truly,

Jno. S. Mosby[7]

Slemp was the only one, of the three men running congressional races, to win. In the presidential race Theodore Roosevelt easily defeated respected attorney Alton Brooks Parker. Mosby, in another jab at Col. William Chapman and his wife, Josie, sarcastically asked whom Josie had voted for. In reality, since women still did not have the vote, he was asking for whom William Chapman would be voting—with Josie's approval, of course.

1. U.S. marshal in the Staunton, Virginia, District Office.
2. Mosby's August 18, 1894, letter in the Staunton newspaper was a discourse on the plight of the Negro and the impact in the current presidential race. It was published as an open letter to his friend Sam Chapman.
3. George A. Revercomb was a Virginia state senator as well as Sam Chapman's son-in-law. He was running against incumbent Henry D. "Hal" Flood for Virginia's Tenth District congressional seat.
4. Mitchell, *Letters,* 317; Park Agnew, a leader of one faction of the Virginia Republican Party.
5. Col. Campbell Slemp was the incumbent Republican congressman from Virginia's Ninth District.
6. S. Harris Hoge lost his bid for the Sixth District seat against Rep. Carter Glass. Hoge was also unsuccessful in his later bid for Virginia governor in 1923.
7. GLC 3921.07. John Mosby. Autograph letter signed: to Sam Chapman, 10 September 1904 (The Gilder Lehrman Collection, courtesy of The Gilder Lehrman Institute of American History, New York).

"He Spoke Kindly of You"

Colonel Mosby continued to advise his friend on possible political appointments.

Jany. 14th 1905   Department of Justice
                                   Washington

Dear Sam:

Last night I went to John Daniel's house to see him on
business. This is the first time I have called on anyone this
winter & I went on a very urgent matter. He spoke kindly of
you & said that there is a provision for a lot of new faces in
the Interior Dept. & thinks you can get one. Said he would
send me the bill today with the item marked. If he does I shall
forward it to you. Revercomb better write to Daniel & Slemp
about it. Willie Mosby just left here. He says he thinks he can
get you a place under Agnew which will suit you much better
than one on the "provinces." The enclosed letter you can keep.
It is from Gen. Rucker one of Forrest's generals. He married
my cousin. I will not be here next week.

                                   Very truly
                                   Jno. S. Mosby[1]

Mosby urged Sam to have Revercomb, his son-in-law, write to his
political officeholders. Willie Mosby, Colonel Mosby's brother, was
postmaster in Bedford, Virginia. Agnew was a leader in the Republican Party of Virginia. In speaking of the "provinces" Mosby was likely
referring to the outlying regions in the Interior Department's Land
Management Office, where he had once worked.

1. GLC 3921.09. John Mosby. Autograph letter signed: to Sam Chapman, 14 January 1905 (The Gilder Lehrman Collection, courtesy of The Gilder Lehrman Institute of American History, New York).

"Controversies over Patronage"

The Colonel's patience with trying to find a position for Sam Chapman,
then almost sixty-seven years old, finally ran out following receipt of
a letter from Sam in response to a suggestion that Sam might have to
take a storekeeper's place if he was to work for the government.

Mch. 1st 1905   Department of Justice
                                       Washington

Dear Sam:

    Your letter recd. You speak of Fount's letter to you about
your accepting a storekeeper's place as knowing his mind is
in a state of eclipse. I don't think so. He only suggested it as
the best thing Agnew could do for you as nearly all the other
places are in the Classified Service. Some very good men have
been [illegible], i.e., Robert [illegible], Col. Samuel Berkley,
(8th Va.) was a storekeeper in Alex[andria] during Cleveland's
first term. I recommended him to be retained under Harrison.
I did not receive the letter which you say you wrote me in
Alabama. You speak of the place I "vacated" as Special Agent.
I never vacated a place as Special Agent. The law does not
fix the number of Special Agents, in fact says nothing about
Special Agents. It only appropriates a lump sum of money
to be used by the Secretary in protecting public lands. He is
invested with a large discretion in using it for that end. He
may employ one or a hundred agents—or none. I did go with
you to see the Secretary. He was away. I gave the papers to,
and talked with, his secretary, in your presence about you.
Afterward, Charlie Pollard sent me a letter from U.S. District
Attorney Rowland of Birmingham addressed to the President
recommending my friend Charlie Pollard of Alabama to be a
Special Agent. John Daniel & Pollard have been schoolmates
& friends. I wrote to John Daniel & asked him to [speak] to
the Secty. of the Interior about Pollard. He did not do it, I
suppose because the Presidential Campaign was going on. I
did endorse & send Rowland's letter to the President. There
was no more inconsistency in this than my recommending at
the same time yourself & Wm. Chapman to be postal clerks.
You were both appointed. You & Pollard might have been
both appointed. The Commissioner told you that you were
too old. Charlie Pollard would not accept the place if required
to go outside of Alabama. The Secretary told me last October
that he would not let a Special Agent serve in the State from
which he is appointed. So that put Charlie Pollard out. I can

see no inconsistency in Daniel's recommending both you & Pollard to be Special Agents. But Pollard does not want it—he would not leave his family to go outside of Alabama. None of the Special Agents have been detailed to go to Alabama to continue the work I was doing. I do not think you ought to have been surprised at Daniel's preferring his old schoolmate to anybody, especially as it did you no harm. Pollard was not appointed. Daniel did give you his endorsement. What more could he have done? I had really forgotten that Charlie Pollard had ever been recommended to be a Special Agent for he long ago abandoned the idea. So John is free to recommend you. What did he go with you to the Land Office for if not to recommend your appointment. He has never recommended Pollard. If I were in his place I would recommend you both. I did tell you that I thought it wd. be useless to go to the White House as Special Agents are appointed by the Dept. It is true that I was appointed at McKinley's request—that was because he knew me personally. I hear that Slemp will try to oust Agnew. I had an interview with the President last week to report on Alabama matters. When leaving I said to him—"I hope Agnew will not be defeated—he is one of the best men in Va." I have no idea of mingling anymore in controversies over patronage. I wish I never had. In justice to Fount I ought to say that I first suggested to him to write to you & make the offer. I have in my life recd. several fees much higher than my whole year's salary is now. Pulling down fences is not as dignified as arguing cases in the Supreme Court. I have done both.

Very truly
Jno. S. Mosby[1]

In what was probably his severest letter to a close confidant such as Sam Chapman, John Mosby appeared to let out all his frustrations over patronage hiring. This was notable in the last few sentences when he referred to his own positions within the government. He also admitted that it was he—not Fount Beattie—who suggested Sam take a storekeeper's appointment.

1. GLC 3920.10. John Mosby. Autograph letter signed: to Sam Chapman, 1 March 1905 (The Gilder Lehrman Collection, courtesy of The Gilder Lehrman Institute of American History, New York).

Sam Gets a Job and Mosby Finds a Lost Book

John Mosby was in Joe Bryan's office at the *Richmond Times* when he wrote Sam and broke the news that the book for which he had been searching for ten years was found. He now had something tangible on which to place his defense of General Stuart's actions during the Gettysburg campaign.

Dec. 23rd 1905   Joseph Bryan
Capt. Sam Chapman   Richmond, Va.

Dear Sam:

I have just seen L. L. Lewis[1] who told me that he had a letter from Sam Yost[2] saying that you had got an appointment under Brown Allen.[3] It is not necessary for me to tell you how delighted I am. Joe Bryan is sitting by me—he sends his love & congratulations. I have at last found what I have been looking for [for] 10 years. It is Gen. Lee's letter book on the Gettysburg Campaign. Good old McCabe[4] has it. It confirms all that I have written in defense of Stuart & reputes the calumnies against him. I will explain all when I see you.

Yours Truly
Jno. S. Mosby[5]

Mosby used the book in his defense of General Stuart when he wrote *Stuart's Cavalry in the Gettysburg Campaign* (1908).

1. Judge Lansford L. Lewis was a former president of the Virginia Supreme Court of Appeals and a friend of President Theodore Roosevelt.
2. Maj. Samuel M. Yost, a Confederate veteran and past owner and publisher of several Staunton area newspapers. He was also Staunton postmaster.
3. U.S. marshal in the Staunton District Office.
4. Carmichael, *Lee's Young Artillerist;* close friend of Joe Bryan. Captain

McCabe was a college classmate and intimate friend, as well as adjutant to Colonel Pegram when Pegram was killed in April 1865.
5. GLC 3921.12. John Mosby. Autograph letter signed: to Sam Chapman, 23 December 1905 (The Gilder Lehrman Collection, courtesy of The Gilder Lehrman Institute of American History, New York).

Longstreet the Soldier—Unjustly Censured

With the help of Colonel Mosby, Senator John Daniel, and others, Sam Chapman was situated as a deputy U.S. marshal in the Western District of Virginia with headquarters in Staunton. The city was about eighty miles from Sam's home in Covington, so he set up housekeeping in a rented house with his youngest daughter, Mary.[1]

March 7th 1906 Department of Justice
Washington

Dear Sam:

Your letter recd. Please ask Major Yost to send me a half dozen copies of the paper with his article. I am glad that you preserve your friendly relations with him & hope you will not identify yourself with his & Brown Allen's quarrel. I suppose you are now safe in your position. Understand that I find no fault with Longstreet[2] the soldier but with Longstreet the historian. No man, except Stuart, was ever more unjustly censured than Longstreet has been at Gettysburg. He committed no fault there. In criticizing Stuart he only followed Gen. Lee's report—he thought it was right. He had forgotten his order to Stuart to do the very thing that he criticized him for doing. It is true that in reply to him I published his order to Stuart (1887). But having made the charge he stuck to it when he wrote his book (1896).

Yours truly
Jno. S. Mosby[3]

Colonel Mosby was resolute in his loyalty to the memory of his former mentor, Gen. Jeb Stuart. But he was probably in the minority in his defense of General Longstreet at Gettysburg. It is unknown what quarrel Sam Yost had with Brown Allen.

1. Brown, *Mosby's Fighting Parson*, 341.
2. Gen. James Longstreet, one of Lee's corps commanders; he played a pivotal role at Gettysburg.
3. Stuart-Mosby Historical Society Collection.

Mosby in New England

Colonel Mosby had returned from Boston, where he was the honored guest and speaker at the birthday celebration of his friend the late president U. S. Grant.

———

May 9th 1906   Department of Justice
                                      Washington

Dear Sam:

As I write the date of this letter I am reminded that about this time 43 years ago you were surrounding the 1st West Va. Cavalry regiment at Warrenton Junction.[1]—I returned on Tuesday from Boston. I had a perfect ovation there. Two Union soldiers whom we captured came to Providence to meet me. They took me all over Massachusetts to historic spots—Bunker Hill—Faneuil Hall—Lexington—Concord—Cambridge—Plymouth Rock—& to Marshfield, Daniel Webster's home. You know I have always been not only an admirer but an idolater of Webster. At the Grant banquet I sat between my two former prisoners. They came to the train to see me off. Each brought a token of friendship with them. The first day I was in Boston I felt sorry that I had ever captured these two men. They showed so much kindness to me. After that I felt sorry they did not capture me. At the train when parting I said that I never could forget their kindness. One—Captain Barton—replied "We have not half paid the debt owed you for your kindness to us." I sent you a paper with the short speech I made at the banquet. If you had heard the

applause when I concluded you wd. have thought there was
an earthquake in Boston. I do not think I said a word about
Grant or Lee that any Southern or Northern fair minded man
wd. not endorse. Judge Bruce,[2] who lives at Walden, 6 miles
from Boston took me home with him to dinner & I spent the
night there—The Governor and the Secretary of State came out
to the dinner on an automobile.[3] The next morning Captain
Barton—my former prisoner—drove me back to Boston.
We stopped at Harvard to see Mrs. Webster—the daughter
of Major Forbes (now dead) whom we captured.[4] She and
her husband were all kindness. I suppose I mentioned that I
was going to Concord & Lexington as I recd. from her that
evening a nice letter enclosing a note of introduction to her
Aunt—Miss Emerson, the daughter of Ralph Waldo Emerson,
who lives at their old home in Concord. Sunday we drove
to Lexington & Concord along the same road on wch. Paul
Revere took his midnight ride to warn the farmers that the
British were coming. We spent several hours at Lexington—
recd. a great deal of attention & dined with an old Union
soldier. Then we drove on—six miles—to Concord—stopped
at the Emerson home on the outskirts of the town & presented
my letter of introduction. Miss Emerson had recd. a note from
her niece telling her I was coming & she was expecting me.
She recd. me cordially & took me to her father's studio. Of
course it was interesting to me. I am familiar with Emerson's
writings & I have read his life by Dr. Holmes.[5] My memory
seemed to recall all I had read connected with him. I told her
that I had all my life been reading & repeating her father's ode
on the unveiling of the Concord monument & that I wanted
to read it in the room where it was written. So she handed me
the volume that had the poem. I opened it—a gentleman asked
me to read it aloud wch. I did—It begins "By the rude bridge
that arched the flood, Their flag to April's breeze unfurled, tis
here the embattled farmers stood, And fired the shot heard
round the world."[6] I read it with deep feeling for I felt it. I
had just finished reading it when Mrs. Webster & her husband
came in. They thought I wd. be there & had driven 10 miles to
see me. Then we drove on to Concord bridge where the fight

began & the monument stands. To me Lexington & Concord are the two most interesting places I ever was at. They made a deep impression on me. When a child I read about them in Peter Parley[7]—but never expected to see them & then I was overwhelmed with kindness. On Saturday we went down to Marshfield, Daniel Webster's home & also to Plymouth Rock. Of course any place associated with Daniel Webster is interesting to me. The lady at the house showed me his powder horn & a pair of pants in the old style of flaps wch. he wore about the farm. I sat in the chair in wch. he meditated his great orations. We then went to the family burying ground. Only the Webster family is buried there. There is a turfed oval mound about 4 feet high & a marble slab of the same height over Webster. It's simplicity is befitting the great man who sleeps under it. As I stood by Webster's tomb I involuntarily repeated Milton's lines on Shakespeare's:

"What needist my Shakspeare to be laid beneath a star pointing pyramid?

x   x   x   x   x   x

And so sepulchred in such pomp doth lie, that kings for such a tomb might wish to die."[8]

We also went to Plymouth—not far from Marshfield & I stood on the Rock where the Pilgrims landed from the Mayflower. I do not believe in their theology & long prayers— Their hell fire & damnation—yet they were a noble bunch of heroes inspired by lofty motives & are worthy of the praise of Mrs. Hemans'[9] hymn. I forgot to mention that one of the most interesting characters I met was an old fisherman who told me that he had often gone out in a boat with Daniel Webster fishing. I wished I was the fisherman. I hope my visit to Boston will do good. You can let Major Yost & Hugh McIlhany read this letter.

Yours truly,
Jno. S. Mosby[10]

I forgot to mention that I had been only a few minutes in

Faneuil Hall before the champagne bottles began to pop. I wonder what the Pilgrims wd. have thought of that?

———

1. Brown, *Mosby's Fighting Parson*, 117–19; on May 3, 1863, Mosby and about ninety-eight partisans struck the train depot at Warrenton Junction, Virginia, capturing three hundred men and officers before being routed by a large contingent of the Fifth New York and First Vermont Cavalries, losing most of their prisoners and barely escaping themselves. Mosby counted three Rangers mortally wounded and several captured.

2. Mitchell, *Letters*, 144–45, Charles M. Bruce, chairman of the executive committee that invited Mosby to speak.

3. Governor Curtis Guild Jr. and Secretary William M. Olin.

4. Brown, *Mosby's Fighting Parson*, 181–83, on July 6, 1863, Mosby's Rangers fought a bitter battle with Maj. William H. Forbes and portions of the Second Massachusetts and Thirteenth New York Cavalries. The Union troopers were badly beaten and Forbes was captured. After the war, Mosby became close friends with Forbes and his family.

5. Dr. Oliver W. Holmes (1809–1894) wrote a biography of Ralph Waldo Emerson (1803–1882); it was first published in 1885. Dr. Holmes was the father of Oliver Wendell Holmes, the noted jurist.

6. Ralph Waldo Emerson, "Concord Hymn," *The Oxford Book of American Verse*, ed. F. O. Matthiessen (Oxford: Oxford University Press, 1952), 69; Mosby has used "tis here" in the third line; the actual wording is "here once."

7. American Web Books.com, *Tales of Peter Parley about America*, http://www.americanwebbooks.com/book.php. This was the first in a series of books, for children, published from 1828 through the turn of the twentieth century.

8. Mosby is quoting *John Milton on Shakespeare*.

9. Public Domain Music, http://www.pdmusic.org/hymns, Mrs. Felicia Dorethea Hemans (1794–1835), "The Tyrolese Evening Hymn" (1828).

10. Fauquier Historical Society Collection.

"It Only Shows His Obtuse Sensibility"

John Mosby's position in the Justice Department left him with more than enough time on his hands to write, travel, and lecture. He had recently returned from a speaking engagement in Boston. But he was offended by a letter from a former Confederate officer.

———

May 9th 1906   Department of Justice
                                              Washington

Dear Sam:

Herewith is a copy of a letter I wrote Bev[1] giving him an outline of my Boston trip. Show it to Yost & McIlhany.[2] If you ever get to Lexington let Scott Shipp[3] read it. Joe Bryan writes me that McCabe did not mean to insult me by writing me a letter abusing Grant & when nothing had been said by anyone to provoke such a letter—but just the reverse. I had not written to McCabe—only sent him a paper [illegible]. Now, I have no idea that he intended to insult me—it only shows his obtuse sensibility. I wd. be very obtuse if I were not offended by it. Any real gentleman wd. know that such a letter wd. offend me.

                                              Yours truly
                                              Jno. S. Mosby[4]

———

It is surprising that Mosby would get so upset with Gordon McCabe, the former Confederate ("good old McCabe") who, just a few months before, shared General Lee's letter book—the one for which Mosby had searched for the past ten years—with Mosby. However, as with Stuart, Colonel Mosby was very defensive when it came to criticism of his friend Grant.

    1. Beverly Mosby, Colonel Mosby's son.
    2. Hugh McIlhany, former member of Mosby's command.
    3. Superintendent of V.M.I.; commandant of cadets at New Market Battle, May 1864.
    4. GLC 3921.14. John Mosby. Autograph letter signed: to Sam Chapman, 9 May 1906 (The Gilder Lehrman Collection, courtesy of The Gilder Lehrman Institute of American History, New York).

"Joe Is Running a Bloody Shirt Newspaper"

While he was in Boston, John Mosby had written to his close friend and former Ranger Joe Bryan, publisher of the *Richmond Times*. Apparently Bryan was disturbed by the favorable manner in which the

Colonel described the New Englanders, for he, Bryan, was not in a state of forgiveness to his former enemies.

———

May 19th 1906   Department of Justice
Captain Sam Chapman   Washington

Dear Sam—
    Very glad to get your letter—sorry about the disaster to the printing press. There never was published anything I wrote that the printer did not mutilate it. In the sentence in my speech about Caius Marius the printer interlopes "one" after "but not"—& then a "the" before Caius Marius.[1] Still on the whole it is well done & thank Sam Yost for me. Joe's letter to me does not express his real sentiments—In his reply he shows that he regrets writing such a letter to me for it was uncalled for. I had said nothing about politics—the war—or forgiving anybody. He sent me with a very affectionate answer a letter he had just recd. from a Union soldier in Boston who spoke of his treatment by the Confederates at their reunion in New Orleans. Joe said he wanted to show me "that all generosity was not on one side." I wrote back that I had made no concessions only spoke of the hospitality shown to me & that I was proud to see that New Orleans had responded so generously to the reception Boston had given me. I did not want to be too hard on Joe, so I will not tell him that the New Orleans people did not practice his code of forgiving Union soldiers, i.e., (1) sorrow for what they did (2) atonement—for I have no idea that their Union soldiers ever expressed sorrow or atonement. The truth is Joe is running a bloody shirt newspaper—he conforms to the sentiments of the paper, the paper does not conform to Joe's. My reception in Boston shows that there is no such code there—nobody ever heard me express sorrow for the side I took in the war—I certainly have made no atonement. Joe concluded his letter by saying he was going to the Episcopal Convention in Alex[andria]. His letter said he could never forgive the Puritans for persecuting. A good deal of my letter to Ben[2]

about the Puritans & the Episcopalians is really an answer
to Joe. If you will read the life of Patrick Henry you will
see how the Episcopalians persecuted the Baptists. I told
Joe that Bob Ingersoll[3] had long ago forgiven the Puritans
although he abhorred their creed. You say you have been
to Abingdon. I went into camp there in May 1861—I shall
leave here for Bedford next Saturday—stop over at the
University. Am always glad to hear from you. My regards to
Sam Yost.

Yours Truly

Jno. S. Mosby[4]

Joe Bryan had taken Colonel Mosby's remarks, in a letter Mosby wrote
to him while in Boston, to mean that Mosby had forgiven the Yankees.
In a reply Mosby said he was not asking Joe to forgive anyone but
only telling him of how he was treated. Bryan's "code for forgiveness": first, expressing sorrow for how the Union had desolated the
South, and second, making an atonement for it, seemed to have gotten
under Mosby's skin. He alluded to this in his reply to Bryan: "Unless I
have been wrong Jesus did not prescribe the conditions of forgiveness
which you require."[5]

1. The plebeian (157–86 B.C.) who professionalized the Roman army, and
who, in doing so, created the military basis of what would become the Roman
Empire. Caius Marius is popularly immortalized in John Vanderlyn's painting
Caius Marius amidst the Ruins in Carthage.

2. Probably Ben Palmer of Richmond, Captain Chapman's lieutenant in
Company B of the Forty-third Battalion and a good friend of both Chapman
and Mosby.

3. Robert (Bob) Ingersoll was notorious in the latter part of the nineteenth century for his assaults on religion and well known as defense counsel
in the Post Office scandals (1882–1883) that resulted in civil service reforms
during President Chester Arthur's administration.

4. Dave Goetz Collection.

5. GLC 3921.15. John Mosby. Autograph letter (typed, 2 pp.) signed: to
Joseph Bryan, 14 May 1906 (The Gilder Lehrman Collection, courtesy The
Gilder Lehrman Institute of American History, New York).

Colonel Smith's Dirge

Colonel Mosby was in Bedford and wrote to Sam on stationery of his brother's drugstore. This letter revealed some of Mosby's seldom seen humorous bent during the last decade of his life.

June 1st 1906   Mosby Drug Co.
                                                Bedford City, Va.

Dear Sam:

Recd. your letter. I leave for Washington on Sunday. Have you read Col. Tom Smith's dirge at Hollywood [Richmond cemetery].[1] It is the song of the dying swan—observe that in the last sentence he bids eternal farewell to "ladies & comrades" saying it is the last reunion he will attend for "ere another" he will "have gone to the banner that has taken its flight to greet the warrior souls." In other words that before another decoration day—May 30th 1907—he will be in Heaven—or somewhere else. (Probably Hugh[2] knows where Tom will be.) He bid an eternal farewell. I have just written Ben to let me know if Col. Tom is in a dying condition—or is contemplating suicide. I also wrote Ben[3] to tell Bob Hunter[4] not to let Col. Tom carry off the Confederate muster rolls wch. he has been collecting & also to take a snapshot of him just before he takes flight. Please tell Sam Yost[5] to have his obituary written.

                                                Yours truly
                                                Jno. S. Mosby[6]

You did not enclose the letter I sent you to read and return.

1. Col. Tom Smith, son of William "Extra Billy" Smith, two-term governor of Virginia. Tom Smith was a Civil War veteran who migrated to New Mexico territory following the war, where he became U.S. attorney and later chief justice of the territory. He delivered the "dying swan's" address, referred to by Mosby, in Capitol Square, Richmond, at the statue previously dedicated to his father. He died in Warrenton, Virginia, on June 29, 1918.
2. Hugh McIlhany.

3. Ben Palmer of Richmond, Captain Chapman's lieutenant in Company B of the Forty-third Battalion and a good friend of both Chapman and Mosby.

4. Maj. Robert Hunter was a friend of both Chapman and Mosby, living in Staunton, Virginia.

5. Staunton, Virginia, newspaper publisher.

6. Fauquier Historical Society Collection.

"The Late City of San Francisco"

Mosby, visiting his brother in Bedford, Virginia, wrote Sam that he had received a letter from Willie Chapman, in San Francisco, about six weeks after the cataclysmic earthquake and fire had devastated the city.

—————

June 7th 1906   Department of Justice
                                                Washington

Dear Sam:

I recd. a letter from you when I was in Bedford saying that you wd. send me the *Old Dominion Sun* that had something of interest to me. It has not come. I had a letter from Willie Chapman a few days ago written from the late city of San Francisco.[1] It is now almost as deserted as Palmyra. I want to pay another visit to Bedford in October & go via Staunton & Lexington. I have not yet heard of the demise of Col. Smith. Tell Sam Yost that as Tom has announced his own death within a certain definite, short time it wd. be perfectly legitimate for him to publish Tom's obituary before he actually dies—just as Dear Swift did that of Partridge—The Almanac maker.[2] My kind regards to Yost & Hugh.[3] I enclosed Tom's speech in a letter to Bev—also your letter. Did Hugh cry when he heard Tom's speech?

Yours Truly,
Jno. S. Mosby[4]

—————

1. On April 18, 1906, a giant earthquake leveled great portions of the city. The water system was destroyed, and less than ten hours later fires broke out. The toll: 500 dead, 30,000 homeless.

2. Jonathan Swift (1667–1745), under the pseudonym Issac Bickerstaff, published an almanac, *Prediction for the Ensuring Year,* in which he foretold the death of John Partridge, a so-called predictor of astrological events, on a certain day in the year. He then publicly affirmed the death on that day. Despite all of Partridge's protestations, it was generally believed he had in fact died as Swift had foretold.

3. Sam Yost, publisher of Staunton area newspapers; Hugh McIlhany, Staunton businessman and former Mosby Ranger.

4. GLC 3921.17. John Mosby. Autograph letter signed: to Sam Chapman, 7 June 1906 (The Gilder Lehrman Collection, courtesy of The Gilder Lehrman Institute of American History, New York).

Colonel Tom and Extra Billy

Colonel Mosby commented on his old political adversaries—Col. Tom Smith and his father, William "Extra Billy" Smith.

———

June 8th 1906   Department of Justice
                                             Washington

Dear Sam:

I met a Texas gentleman yesterday who told me he stood near Tom Smith and heard his speech on decoration day & that the worst part of it was *suppressed*. I shall go over to Alexandria tomorrow & have a laugh with Chinn.[1] Men who profess such hostile sentiments are always the first to pick up the crumbs. I remember when I told him in 1869 that I should vote for Walker and the expurgated Constitution (it was the best constitution Va. ever had and she lived longer under it) how Tom reared up in his stirrups—then when Walker[2] came to Warrenton to speak I introduced him and made a speech, which was exploited in favor of voting for Walker and the Constitution in order to get rid of military government. Doug Tyler[3] was married that day near Upperville—I was invited but did not go as I considered it my duty to stay in Warrenton and set an example—It was a new situation and the people needed leaders. I remarked that I wd. as soon have ridden to the rear when I ordered my men to charge as go off that day; although you know at that time I went to all the weddings. Walker arrived on the 10 O.C. A.M. train—before it came in Gen. Hunton—Gen. Payne—Tom Smith—Jimmy Keith—Aleck Payne started off to the wedding. You know that it looked risky—like taking the plunge at Niagara—to take Walker and the Constitution.[4] Old Extra Billy was called on to speak after Walker finished—He advised the people to vote for Walker—*but against the Constitution.* Now voting against the Constitution was in effect voting to perpetuate [?] military rule. Well, we routed the negroes & carpetbaggers—I never held, or was even a candidate for an office under that constitution—In fact the only thing the State of Va. ever did for me was to keep me locked up eleven months in the Albemarle jail—Maybe I deserved it—but I do not feel the least gratitude for it—(Maybe Hugh thinks I am ungrateful.) Now every one of these gentlemen afterward were candidates for office and took the full benefit of getting reconstructed with the Underwood Constitution. Yet—they refused to run any risks. In 1876–77 Extra was in the Legislature—A resolution was offered to remove Jim Barbour's[5] disability under the anti-dueling law—Mathews of Loudoun offered an amendment to include me—Extra rose and made a bitter speech against me— he carried three votes with him—two were carpetbaggers—I recently met Tip Strother—he was in the Legislature. He spoke of Extra's speech against me—Show this to Sam Yost & Hugh.

Yours Truly
Jno. S. Mosby[6]

When the military authorities in Virginia postponed indefinitely the ratification vote for the Underwood Constitution—and with the election of the Republican candidate for president, U. S. Grant—prominent Conservative leaders petitioned Congress for readmittance of the state into the Union; following Grant's recommendation, Virginia was restored.

1. Benton Chinn, a former Ranger and good friend of Mosby.
2. Woodward, *The Confederacy's Forgotten Son,* 139; Gilbert C. Walker

was a New York carpetbagger who, ironically, had the support of Virginia's Conservative Party, which feared the possible election of H. H. Wells, a member of the Radical Party, comprised mostly of Negroes, scalawags, and carpetbaggers.

3. Stiles, *4th Virginia Cavalry*; Douglas Tyler was a member of the Fourth Virginia Cavalry during the war.

4. Woodward, *The Confederacy's Forgotten Son*, 139; the Underwood Constitution, Virginia's first Reconstruction constitution. It was drawn up primarily by members of the Radical Party, knowing they could get the Negro vote.

5. A Culpeper lawyer, Barbour agreed to be Mosby's "second" in a proposed duel with Alexander (Aleck) Payne. Payne, a politically active attorney, had printed derogatory remarks about Mosby.

6. Michael Macdonald Collection.

"I Don't Suppose Hugh Suffered Much"

Former Ranger Hugh McIlhany of Staunton received the brunt of his former commander's biting sarcasm in this letter. And Mosby again found an opportunity to deride William Chapman's wife and mother-in-law.

————

October 13th 1906   Department of Justice
                                     Washington

Dear Sam:

Herewith a letter from Scott Shipp[1] in reply to one I wrote him congratulating him on being retired on the Carnegie Fund.[2] Incidentally, I explained why I wd. not be at the reunion. I was glad I was not. I couldn't have stood listening to the Rev. Jones. You see Scott Shipp has the same opinion of him that I have. I was amused at Hugh's speech in wch. he recounts the hardships he endured. Now Hugh joined my command in Sept. 1864—he was captured Dec. 21st '64. Was with us three months. I don't suppose Hugh suffered much in the Commissary Dept. where he was until he joined our command.[3] Don't think he could have suffered much in the three months he was with us but the report says his recital of his hardships drew tears. (I wd. have laughed.) Now, (quoting

scripture) he says Mosby's men had neither scrip or purse.[4]
It was during the time Hugh was with us that we made the
Greenback Raid.[5] I think a majority of my men had purses
with greenbacks & that they scattered them freely. I have no
doubt that Hugh had a stomach full when he was captured—
probably some greenbacks. Is it true that the 8th Illinois
proposes a joint reunion? Where will it be? Do you ever see
Sam Yost? My regards to him.

Yours truly,
Jno. S. Mosby[6]

If old Mrs. Jeffries was living I wd. ask you to explain to her
that I was in no way responsible for your picture being in the
Wash. Times & Josie's & Col. William's not being there. I met
a man on the street who introduced himself to me & showed
me the *Times* wch. was just out. Now why it should have your
picture & not Col. Williams I don't know & can't understand.
I do not know anybody connected with the *Times* & they did
not get any pictures from me.

---

1. Superintendent of Virginia Military Institute, Lexington.
2. Reader's Digest Assoc., *Family Encyclopedia,* Andrew Carnegie,
wealthy industrialist and philanthropist, endowed the Carnegie Teacher's Pen-
sion Fund with $10 million in 1905 following the sale of his interests in steel
enterprises to J. P. Morgan.
3. Keen and Mewborn, *43rd Battalion,* 347 (roster); prior to enlisting in
Mosby's command Hugh McIlhany was captain and quartermaster for General Longstreet's First Corps.
4. Bible, King James Version, Matthew 10:9–10: "Provide neither gold,
nor silver, nor brass in your purses, nor script for your journey."
5. Wert, *Mosby's Rangers,* 232–35. On October 14, 1864, Colonel Mosby and eighty-four members of his command derailed a B&O train near Harp-
ers Ferry. They captured two Union paymasters with $168,000. The "spoils"
were divided among the men with the exception of Mosby, who refused any
share. The men used what would have been his to buy their leader a thorough-
bred named Coquette.
6. Horace Mewborn Collection.

"I Am Innocent—Am Not Responsible"

Colonel Mosby still twiddled his thumbs in the Justice Department, spending more time writing letters and trying to accommodate old comrades, while getting an occasional assignment to the Alabama forests and the Western territories. Sam Chapman, serving as a deputy U.S. marshal in Staunton, was involved in a buggy accident.

October 17th 1906   Department of Justice
                                     Washington

Dear Sam:

Your letter recd. Am glad you didn't suffer by your buggy accident as I did in mine.[1] I start for the Indian Territory[2] next Saturday but shall stop over at the University to see Mosby & Spottswood Campbell[3] from Saturday evening until Monday evening. My headquarters will be their room—House B. I want it perfectly understood that I do not go to reunions because the speeches disgust me. Tell the "headless horseman" that I expect to pass through Staunton next Monday evening on the C&O train that leaves Washington at 2 P.M. Remember me to Sam Yost. I suppose you recd. the *Washington Times* I sent you that had your picture. I also sent a copy to Willie. If old Mrs. Jeffries[4] were alive she wd. raise a nose because yours, not Colonel Williams's was there. Really, I am innocent—am not responsible for the printer.

Yours truly
Jno. S. Mosby[5]

1. Jones, *Ranger Mosby*, 303–4. Several years earlier Mosby had been injured when a horse pulling his buggy was startled and kicked him in the face and head, causing him to lose an eye.
2. Siegel, *Rebel*, 276–77; after Mosby's success with the investigation and prosecution of western cowmen violating the Interior Department's Land Lease regulations, he was sent by President Roosevelt, working through the Justice Department, to the Indian territories to investigate the misappropriation of tribal funds.

3. Mosby's grandsons, children of his eldest daughter, May, who died two years earlier.
4. Col. William Chapman's mother-in-law.
5. John T. Kincheloe Collection.

"Eradicating Old Prejudices"

John Mosby returned to Washington following his highly enjoyable trip to Boston, where he spoke to the Boston Middlesex Republication Club on the celebration of Grant's birthday. Feeling in a conciliatory mood, he wrote to friends at the University of Virginia and elsewhere.

————————

November 24th 1906   Department of Justice
                                      Washington

Dear Sam:

I recd. & enjoyed your letter—also the newspaper wch. the "headless horseman" sent me. You remember Mrs. Rhodes, the lady who owns my old home. On my return I sent copies of my Boston trip to her & Frank Smith, who passed it to Dr. Alderman & Prof. Fitzhugh.[1] They professed to be pleased with it & Mrs. Rhodes wrote me in behalf of a number of students to whom she had shown it, asking me to let her publish it in the *Charlottesville Progress*. I consented. Just got a letter from her saying that it will be published in a few days. So look out for it. I consented to the publication because I thought it might do some good & would contribute toward eradicating old prejudices. Scott Shipp was very much pleased with it. I suppose the letter will horrify Hugh by what I said of the Episcopalians. My cousin, George McLaurine (you know what a Baptist he is) was very much pleased as the Episcopal Church in Va. used to persecute Baptists. I say that they treated a Baptist as a Cabel [illegible]. Ask Gordon[2] to tell you what that means in Criminal Law. I suppose my letter will also make Josie mad. The Editor of the *Saturday Mag.* left out in my last article the cream of it. I read your letter with great pleasure. Remember me to Sam Yost.

> Yours Truly,
> Jno. S. Mosby[3]

I sent you under cover a halftone picture of myself wch. I want you to give to Armistead Gordon as recognition of his poem, *Mosby's Men*.[4] I was at the University with his father. What about the Robertsons?[5]

———

1. Smith was a former professor at the University of Virginia; Dr. Alderman was the university president and Fitzhugh a teacher.
2. Armistead Gordon was a former mayor and commonwealth's attorney of Staunton and a renowned poet and author.
3. GLC 3921.19. John Mosby. Autograph letter signed: to Sam Chapman, 24 November 1906 (The Gilder Lehrman Collection, courtesy of The Gilder Lehrman Institute of American History, New York).
4. Armistead Gordon of Staunton had composed the poem "Mosby's Men," which was read at the seventh reunion of the Forty-third Battalion at Fairfax Courthouse in 1900.
5. The Robertsons befriended Colonel Mosby while he was in San Francisco.

Jefferson Davis and the Trial That Wasn't

Mosby attempted to contact old friends from his San Francisco days. His thoughts turned to "Colonel Tom's ridiculous speech" at Hollywood Cemetery, and he again emphasized that Jefferson Davis never stood trial.

———

December 7th 1906   Department of Justice
                                     Washington

Dear Sam:

I have recd. a letter from Mr. Armistead Gordon asking me to write on the picture I gave him that I did in recognition of his poem. I am mailing him one with the inscription. I have heard that my cousin Alice Mosby Gardner is spending the winter in Covington. She thinks a great deal of you & I want you to go see her & also take my cousins to see her. I wd. also like for her to get acquainted with the wife of the doctor (I can't recall the name) I knew in San Francisco who is now in Covington. If you should see the Robertsons, can't you in a gentle way find out why he & not she answered my letter. He had never done such a thing before. In his letter he did not even mention Mrs. Robertson or Mrs. Macon & he knew that I thought a great deal of both. Hence I concluded there must be a separation. Robertson must have lost his position in the Santa Cruz Powder Co. They were always very kind to me. Make Alice laugh about "The Headless Horseman." She will appreciate the humor. Joe Bryan was here a few days ago. I spoke of Colonel Tom's ridiculous speech (May 30th) at Hollywood when in his tragic manner he said it wd. be his last—that he was about to take his flight to mansions in the skies; yet he has made several such speeches since & is still kicking. Joe[1] said that he never read these speeches. I asked him why did he want me to go to these reunions & have to go through the crucifixion of hearing speeches that he couldn't read. But I read both Hugh's & Tom's. Did Robertson read Davis' trial in Chase's Decisions—He speaks from his "recollection." When I heard of John Goode's ridiculous speech I remembered all about the trial (Dec. 1868) but got the book from the library—showed it to several who heard Goode[2] & I wanted to contradict him by the record. Then I wrote to you. There was no decision—or allusion to—about State's Rights or Secession. The indictment was dismissed on the ground that, a few days after the case was argued, the President[3] issued a Proclamation of Pardon. The case ended there. So says the record. Yesterday was my birthday—73.

Yours Truly,
Jno. S. Mosby[4]

Ben Palmer writes me that the Stuart Statue will be unveiled next May 30th. I am now at work on my *Stuart's Cavalry in the Gettysburg Campaign* wch., I want to publish shortly before the unveiling.

Mosby reiterated his disdain for reunions. (The initial reunion of his former command, held in Alexandria in 1895, was the only one he attended.) In this letter the Colonel took John Goode to task for a speech Goode had given relative to the "trial" of Jefferson Davis in 1868. Mosby made his case against Goode's statements by documenting that Jefferson Davis was never tried for treason.

1. Joe Bryan, publisher of the *Richmond Times*; former Ranger and friend to Colonel Mosby.
2. Goode was a native of Bedford County, Virginia, and had a long record of government service. He served in the U.S. Congress from 1875 to 1881.
3. Andrew Johnson.
4. GLC 3921.20. John Mosby. Autograph letter signed: to Sam Chapman, 7 December 1906 (The Gilder Lehrman Collection, courtesy of The Gilder Lehrman Institute of American History, New York).

Patriarchy, Polygamy, Circumcision—and Slavery

Sam Chapman had been in Richmond attending the United Confederate Veterans reunion May 30 through June 3, 1907. Upon Sam's return to Staunton, Mosby wrote to him concerning some of the speeches that were made. Mosby also chronicled the political history of slavery prior to the Civil War, revealing an impressive knowledge of the subject. He candidly recounts his own family's participation in the institution:

June 4th 1907   Department of Justice
                                        Washington

Dear Sam:

I suppose you are now back in Staunton. I wrote you about my disgust at reading the Reunion speeches. It has since been increased by reading Christian's report.[1] I am certainly glad I wasn't there. According to Christian the Virginia people were the abolitionists & the Northern people were pro-slavery. He said slavery was a "patriarchal" institution. So were polygamy & circumcision. Ask Hugh if he has ever been circumcised.

Christian quotes what the old Virginians said against slavery.
True, but why didn't he quote what the modern Virginians
said in favor of it—Mason, Hunter, Wise, etc.[2] Why didn't he
state that a Virginia Senator (Mason) was the author of the
Fugitive Slave Law & why didn't he quote the Virginia Code
(1860) that made it a crime to speak against slavery or to teach
a Negro to read the Lord's Prayer. Now, while I think as badly
of slavery as Horace Greeley[3] did, I am not ashamed that my
family were slave holders. It was our inheritance. Neither am
I ashamed that my ancestors were pirates & cattle thieves.
People must be judged by the standards of their age. If it was
right to own slaves as property it was right to fight for it. The
South went to war on account of Slavery. South Carolina went
to war—as she said in her Secession Proclamation—because
slavery wd. not be secure under Lincoln. South Carolina
ought to know what was the cause for her seceding. The truth
is the modern Virginians debated from the teachings of the
Fathers. John C. Calhoun's[4] last speech had a bitter attack
on Mr. Jefferson for his amendment to the Ordinance of '87
prohibiting slavery in the Northwest Territory. Calhoun was
in a dying condition—was too weak to read it. So James M.
Mason, a Virginia Senator, read it in the Senate about two
weeks before Calhoun's death—Mch. 1850. Mason & Hunter
not only voted against the admission of California (1850) as
a Free State but offered a protest against it wch. the Senate
refused to record on its Journal. Now in the Convention wch.
Gen. Taylor has called to form a Constitution for California,
there were 51 Northern & 50 Southern men—but it was
unanimous against slavery—but the Virginia Senator, with Ran
Tucker[5] & Co., were opposed to giving local self-government
to California. Ask Sam Yost to give Christian a skinning. I am
not ashamed of having fought on the side of slavery—a soldier
fights for his country—right or wrong—he is not responsible
for the political merits of the cause he fights in. The South
was my country. In Fby. 1860 Jeff Davis offered a bill in the
Senate wch. passed making all the territories slave territory.
(See Davis' book) He was opposed to letting the people decide
whether or not they would have slavery—Wm. A. Smith,

President of Randolph-Macon, quit his duties as a teacher &
in 1857–8–9–60 traveled all over Virginia preaching slavery &
proving it was right by the Bible.

Yours Truly
Jno. S. Mosby[6]

Senator Jas. M. Mason was the author of the Fugitive Slave
Law of 1850 but the Ordinance of 1787, for the government
of the Northwest Territory, contained in its amended form, as
passed, the Fugitive Slave Provision. See Benton's *Thirty Years,*
p. 133. [This last paragraph was written on the back of the
envelope.]

---

1. Judge George L. Christian, a Richmond lawyer, was a Confederate
veteran and historian for the United Confederate Veterans (UCV). His report at the reunion, on the causes of the war, upset Mosby, who was in total
disagreement.
2. "Biographical Directory of the U.S. Congress," http://bioguide.con-
gresds.gov. James Murray Mason (1798–1871), member of U.S. Congress
(1837–1839) and U.S. Senate (1847–1861); Robert Mercer T. Hunter (1809–
1887), member of U.S. Congress (1837–1843; 1845–1847) and U.S. Senate
(1847–1861); Henry E. Wise (1806–1876), member of U.S. Congress (1833–
1844) and Virginia governor (1856–1860).
3. Horace Greeley (1811–1872), founder and editor of the *New York Tri-
bune* (1841), was an outspoken abolitionist; he deserted the Whig Party and
was active in founding the Republican Party prior to Lincoln's presidency. He
ran unsuccessfully against Grant for president in 1872.
4. Calhoun (1782–1850), a South Carolina politician, served in many
offices in the U.S. government and as his state's senior senator; in 1850, he
preached long and hard for sovereignty of the states and states' freedom to
pursue their own economic and social interests unchallenged by a national
government.
5. John Randolph "Ran" Tucker, five term congressman and professor of
law at Washington & Lee University in Virginia.
6. GLC 3921.21 John Mosby. Autograph letter signed: to Sam Chapman,
4 June 1907 (The Gilder Lehman Collection, courtesy of The Gilder Lehrman
Institute of American History, New York).

"A Lying Concert between Them"

Colonel Mosby had completed his *Stuart's Cavalry in the Gettysburg Campaign* and was preparing it for publication. He alluded to serious accusations relative to the higher echelon of the Confederate command involving members of General Lee's personal staff, and to A. P. Hill's responsibility in the failure of the campaign.

August 24th 1907   Department of Justice
                                    Washington

Dear Sam:

In my letter yesterday I forgot to tell you to send me the circular sailing list of the steamships. I want to write to Willie[1] but do not want my letters to be stale when he gets them. I shall go to Bedford in October stopping at Charlottesville, Staunton, Lexington, & Lynchburg. Hope to see you at some of these places. I have finished my book & it is now being typed over. I want to send Macmillan a clear copy. It will be ready for them next week. I don't spare General Lee's staff officers. There was a lying concert between them. I mean Marshall, Long, & Taylor.[2] I reconstructed the Gettysburg campaign. Tell Mr. Gordon[3] to load himself up on States' Rights before I come. Did he ever read John Baldwin's testimony before the Reconstruction Committee in wch., in answer to a question, Baldwin[4] said that he & all Confederates had committed treason? I say the Confederates who deny they were rebels are ashamed of it. I am proud of it. What's the difference. I suppose Jim Wiltshire[5] & Stacy Bispham[6]—who married nieces of A. P. Hill[7]—will be mad. I demonstrated that Hill's rashness was the cause of the disaster.[8] My health is better than it ever was. Regards to Hugh.[9]

Yours Truly
Jno. S. Mosby[10]

Even though he had long since departed California, Colonel Mosby cherished his relationship with Willie Chapman, who was still sailing the western Pacific as purser for an Asian steamship company. Mosby surmised that two former members of his command, who married nieces of Gen. A. P. Hill, would not be pleased with his criticism of their wives' uncle in his examination of Gettysburg. General Hill and Gen. Henry Heth were severely taken to task for their actions on July 1 that precipitated the ensuing three days battle when they engaged the enemy at Gettysburg. Mosby also had harsh judgments of General Lee's aides—Col. Charles Marshall and Col. Walter H. Taylor, and to a lesser degree, Col. Armistead L. Long—for, in Mosby's opinion, failing to make known or to make use of information and dispatches that were pertinent to the final assessment of the campaign and General Stuart's role in it. Mosby hinted at the possibility of a friendly exchange with Armistead Gordon, relative to the question of states rights, when he took notice of a fellow Southerner's testimony before the postwar Reconstruction Committee.

1. Willie Chapman.

2. Col. Charles Marshall, Col. Walter H. Taylor, and Col. Armistead L. Long.

3. Staunton, Virginia, lawyer, politician, and poet.

4. John Brown Baldwin (1820–1873), Virginia politician before the war, served in the Confederate Army and in the Confederate Congress. The Reconstruction Act (actually there were several, 1867–1868) passed by the U.S. Congress, imposed strict rule over the former Confederate states and their citizens by forming military districts, disfranchising former Confederate officers and officials, and enfranchising freedmen.

5. Keen and Mewborn, *43rd Battalion*, 384 (roster), Lt. James Wiltshire, a former Ranger, was a physician living in Baltimore.

6. Ibid., Stacy Budd Bispham served as a private in Sam Chapman's Company E.

7. Faust, *Encyclopedia of the Civil War*, 360–61. Gen. Ambrose Powell Hill served as a corps commander when General Lee reorganized the army following the death of Stonewall Jackson in May 1863. General Hill was killed in April 1865, only one week before the surrender of Lee's army at Appomattox. He was the brother of Gen. Daniel Harvey Hill.

8. Mitchell, *Decisive Battles*, 138–50; Faust, *Encyclopedia of the Civil War*, 305, 358. General Hill along with his division commander, Gen. Henry Heth, was responsible for the fight on July 1, 1863, that precipitated the three-day-long battle at Gettysburg.

9. Hugh McIlhany of Staunton, Virginia.

10. (Copy) Fauquier Historical Society Collection.

"Vindictiveness . . . by the Virginia People"

Colonel Mosby was again into a discussion of Jefferson Davis and his "non-trial." He also discussed the disabilities under the Fourteenth Amendment to the U.S. Constitution. Governor William "Extra Billy" Smith, a member of the Virginia House of Delegates, opposed Mosby's exclusion from the disability he was under because of the state's anti-dueling law. But perhaps the biggest affront to Mosby was his not being asked to deliver the address at the unveiling of the statue of his friend and mentor General Stuart in Richmond.

Sept. 5th 1907   Department of Justice
                                                 Washington

Dear Sam:

The Schoolmistress is all wrong; in June 1865 (see War Records) Gen. Lee applied for a pardon—Grant endorsed—Andy Johnson refused it.[1] On Dec. 25th 1868 Johnson issued a proclamation of universal amnesty & pardon—a Christmas gift—Grant had just been elected & he wanted to deprive Grant of the pleasure. Mr. Davis' trial began that month but the Proclamation of Pardon ended it. (See U.S. Statutes-at-Large & Chase's Circuit Court Decisions reported by Bradley Johnson.) Soon after Grant came in he recommended that the Congress pass an act relieving everybody of the disability of the 14th Amendment—a different thing from a pardon for treason. When I came out for Grant in 1872 I told him if he wd. get Congress to pass an act relieving our leading public men of political disability—not from voting, only for holding office—I thought we could carry Virginia for him. He said he wd. try. In a few days Ben Butler[2] introduced & passed a bill that relieved everybody—including Gen. Hunton. Hunton immediately announced himself a Confederate for congress & was elected. I could have had no selfish motive on this as I was never under the disability of the 14th Amendment. I did incur the disability under the Va. Anti-dueling law either to vote or hold office. In 1877 Wm. F. Gordon of Louisa (uncle

of Armistead) introduced a bill to relieve Jim Barbour[3] of
the disability of the anti-dueling law. Matheson of Loudoun
proposed an amendment to include me. Gov. Smith ("Extra")
was a member of the House—he made a bitter speech against
including me. The bill passed. In June 1875 the Democrats
elected Andy Johnson. Judge Caldwell had a glowing eulogy
of him in *The Index*. I wrote a letter to *The Index* wch.
Moore Blackwell signed inquiring if that was the same Johnson who
made a speech to a crowd at the front door of the White
House saying that treason must be made odious by hanging
the traitors & who offered a reward of $100,000 for Jefferson
Davis under the charge of procuring the assassination of
Lincoln. Gordon can show you the Statutes at Large (1865),
the Amnesty Proclamation, & Grant's message on Amnesty in
the President's Messages. I sent my MS—*Stuart's Cavalry in
the Gettysburg Campaign*—to the Macmillan Co. last week.
Have not heard from them. There was more vindictiveness
shown to me by the Virginia people for my voting for Grant
than the North showed to me for fighting four years against
them. I was in Warrenton last week—talked with Judge
Keith—he is now in Staunton. I wish you wd. ask him the
reason why I was not invited to deliver the address at the
unveiling of Stuart's statue. I am the only Virginian who followed
Stuart who named a child after him & I am the only Virginian
who ever published a word in defense of him. The man selected
was one of Stuart's couriers. Then write me what Keith says.

Yours Truly, John S. Mosby[4]

I have no objection to your letting Hugh & Mr. Gordon read
this. Referring to George Christian's eulogy of slavery because
it was a patriarchal institution I reminded you that Polygamy
& Circumcision were patriarchal institutions. I forgot to say
that Eunuchy was also a patriarchal institution. Ask Hugh if I
am right.

Several proclamations of pardon or amnesty were issued by President
Johnson between May 1865 and December 1868. The initial one con-

tained fourteen classes of persons who were excepted (not eligible), for example, West Point graduates who served as Confederate officers and ex-Confederate governors. However, Johnson allowed for personal applications for those in the excepted classes who wished to sue (apply) for individual amnesty. A second proclamation, on September 7, 1867, narrowed the number of exceptions to three; this reduced the number of unpardoned people to about three hundred. Johnson's third proclamation, on July 4, 1868, excluded only Jefferson Davis, former president of the Confederacy, John C. Breckinridge, former general and secretary of war for the Confederacy, and Robert E. Lee, former commander of the Army of Northern Virginia. Finally, Christmas day of that year saw Johnson's final amnesty which was "unconditional and without reservation" to all who had participated in the "rebellion." Mosby had come under Virginia's penalty of disability by way of the anti-dueling stature. Disability clauses generally barred a person from holding office and/or voting.

1. President Andrew Johnson.
2. Faust, *Encyclopedia of the Civil War*, 98–99. Benjamin F. Butler was a powerful politician in the Massachusetts legislature. He secured a political generalship in the war but was so incompetent he lost all of his commands. Resigning his commission he reentered political life, serving in the U.S. Congress and as governor of Massachusetts.
3. Siepel, *Rebel*, 187; Ramage, *Gray Ghost*, 279; James Barbour, a Culpeper, Virginia, lawyer and close friend of Mosby, agreed to be Mosby's "second" in an impending duel with Alexander Payne, a Warrenton lawyer. Mosby took offense at derogatory political remarks that Payne had written about him and challenged Payne to a duel. The duel never took place after the interceding of Judge James Keith, a friend of Mosby; both men apologized.
4. GLC 3293. John Mosby. Autograph letter signed: to Sam Chapman, 5 September 1907 (The Gilder Lehrman Collection, courtesy The Gilder Lehrman Institute of American History, New York).

"I Won't Write under Contract"

Mosby, still pursuing publication of his book *Stuart's Cavalry in the Gettysburg Campaign,* received a response from the potential publisher, Moffat, Yard & Co. They wrote that, although it would be of interest to critical students of the period, they "wish[ed] that there were more incidents, sketches of characters and side lights on the personalities of the distinguished and gallant men with whom the book deals."[1]

Oct. 12th 1907   Department of Justice
                                 Washington

Dear Sam:

As I write the date I am reminded that it is the anniversary of the Greenback Raid.[2] Your letter just recd. I have not yet concluded a bargain for publishing *Stuart's Cavalry in the Gettysburg Campaign*. They insist on including in the contract my memoirs. I positively refuse. I won't write under contract. You observe that their reader says that it is a valuable historical document but lacks the romantic element. Of course it does because it is all true. You must go to see my cousins & tell them—also Stockton Terry[3]—that I shall leave on the 16th, stop over two or three days at the University[4] & then go to Lynchburg & Bedford. My cousins are Baptist—you won't object to them on that account. I enclose a copy of another letter to Moffat, Yard & Co. Munson had told them that I was writing a book & they wrote me some months ago that they wd. like to publish it. I wish you wd. tell Stockton Terry that I will stop over in Lynchburg next week.

Yours truly, Jno. S. Mosby[5]

1. GLC 3921.22. John Mosby. Autograph letter signed: to Messrs. Moffat, Yard & Co., 12 October 1907 (The Gilder Lehrman Collection, courtesy of The Gilder Lehrman Institute of American History, New York).
2. The Rangers raided a B&O train on October 14, 1864. They escaped with over $168,000 in currency. Mosby's date of October 12 is incorrect. That was the date the men left camp for the raid.
3. Keen and Mewborn, *43rd Battalion*, 373 (roster), Robert Stockton Terry, color bearer for the Rangers.
4. The University of Virginia, Charlottesville.
5. John T. Kincheloe Collection.

Extra Billy's Defense

Mosby assured Sam that his brother William could stop worrying over the issues raised relative to William's actions in the war. The apparent intent was to relieve William of his position with the Internal Revenue Service; however, the reasoning behind the removal campaign may have been a shot aimed more at Mosby than William.

Nov. 30th 1907   Department of Justice
                                                 Washington

Dear Sam:

Just recd. your letter. Tell Colonel William that he is in no danger. The complaint made no impression on Capers [?].[1] I went with Fount to see him on Wednesday—In a week or so he will give Fount a better position. I am glad you called to see Meade—I have never seen him. His mother was Miss Steger—a first cousin of my mother. My maternal grandmother was a Steger. Yesterday I had a letter from Thos. Hardaway—Commonwealth's attorney of Amelia—his mother & Meade's were sisters. Tomorrow I shall send you the picture of myself—one for Bowen & one for Meade. I shall add a third one for you. I think Harry Tucker found out that he had got hold of a live wire when he tackled me. I had several hot shots in reserve but he retreated before I could fire them. I intended to ask him what he thought of old Extra-Billy Smith's wanting to burn Lynchburg after he heard of Lee's surrender to prevent the Yankees from getting the tobacco there. I was paroled there a few weeks afterward & heard all about it. He called a meeting of the citizens at the foot of the hill on Main Street & spoke to them from the steps leading to Court St. He wanted to set fire to everything—my cousin, John Mosby Speed, replied to Extra's speech & in opposition to burning the town to spite the Yankees. He also wanted to burn the bridge across the river although the Yankees were on the same side of the river the town is. He then fired up an engine & sent it out on the railroad & burned all the bridges as far as Roanoke.

There were no Yankees in that direction. Lomax[2] retreated
to Danville & burned bridges across creeks that a man could
jump over. John Daniel was at home wounded & told me he
heard of Extra's speech in favor of burning Lynchburg to spite
the Yankees. Quaere? If it was wrong for Sheridan to burn
the Shenandoah Valley while we were fighting how could it
be right for Extra to burn Lynchburg after we had stopped
fighting?—You speak of seeing a picture of a lady with whom
John Randolph was in love. Her name was Maria Ward. I
may some day tell you why they didn't marry—Did you know
that Harry Tucker was an applicant for the judgeship when
McDowell was appointed? Judge Keith told me all about
it—but Harry has tried to keep it a secret. He got Keith to go
to Washington see Mr. Roosevelt & beg him for the place.
Does Judge McDowell know it? Harry is very foxy. I was very
much pleased with McDowell's appointment. I was raised a
Henry Clay Whig & am still one. I wish you wd. ask Judge
McDowell if he was at the University of Va. with Bev.[3] Bev was
there with a grandson of Henry Clay & some years ago (1886)
called to see him at Ashland. Write me a long letter. Remember
me to Bowen & tell him that he has my deep sympathy.

Yours Truly, Jno. S. Mosby[4]

A complaint had been made in the newspapers and in Washington and
Boston political circles against the appointment of William Chapman
to a position in the Internal Revenue Service because of his part in
the killing of over two dozen members of Custer's Michigan cavalry
near Berryville, Virginia, in 1864. Colonel Mosby assisted Chapman
in having the complaint dismissed, because the Northerners were in
the process of burning the houses of civilians when attacked by a force
of Rangers led by William and Sam Chapman. William "Extra Billy"
Smith was the state's governor when he went on his burning tirade in
Lynchburg in April 1865. It is not known just why Mosby was offer-
ing sympathy to his lawyer friend Frederick Bowen of Danville.

1. Apparently an official with the Internal Revenue Service, where both
Fount Beattie and William Chapman had long careers.

2. Gen. Lunsford Lomax refused to surrender his forces when General Lee laid down his arms at Appomattox on April 9, 1865. Lomax went into North Carolina, where he joined Gen. Joe Johnston; the armies surrendered there several weeks later.

3. Colonel Mosby's son Beverly graduated from the University of Virginia.

4. Michael Macdonald Collection.

Colonel Mosby Enjoys the Praise for His Book

Colonel Mosby was pleased with a letter praising his book about the Gettsyburg campaign from an "accomplished" soldier.

————————

August 2nd 1908   Department of Justice
                                          Washington

Dear Sam:

Herewith is a letter from Captain Donohue—whom I suppose you know. Please return it to me. It shows what has been in the South the common opinion about Gettysburg. Let Hugh read it. I hope you will go to hear Taft's speech to the Virginia Republicans. I sent you a copy of Maj. Swift's letter about my book. I am informed that he is a West Point graduate—class of 1871—& that he is regarded as one of the most accomplished officers in the Army. For that reason he was made head of the Army War College.

Jno. S. Mosby[1]

————————

Colonel Mosby received a letter from Major Swift[2] the week before he wrote Sam. Swift's letter thanked Mosby for "the contribution you have made to Military History," saying "your book has been a revelation to me in many ways."[3] The Colonel must have established a close relationship with Swift for, about four years later, he wrote to then Colonel Swift: "I feel very lonely here since you left and hope you will soon complete your tour of duty in the Philippines."[4]

1. GLC 3921.23. John Mosby. Autograph letter signed: to Sam Chap-

man, 2 August 1908 (The Gilder Lehrman Collection, courtesy of The Gilder Lehrman Institute of American History, New York).

2. Maj. Eben Swift graduated from West Point, class of 1876, and finished at the Army War College in 1877. He was director of the Army War College for three years, receiving recognition for introducing the famous Staff Ride, which allowed students access to Civil War battlefields to study the battles. He served as commandant at Ft. Leavenworth and was promoted to brigadier general.

3. Mitchell, *Letters*, 154.

4. Ibid., 177.

"I Expose . . . Gen. Lee's Staff Officers"

Sam Chapman continued work as a U.S. marshal and traveled to the various federal courts within the district; he was at Lynchburg when Colonel Mosby wrote this letter. Mosby continued to write newspaper and magazine articles in defense of Gen. Jeb Stuart, most notably regarding Stuart's actions during the Gettysburg campaign. His book on the subject was nearing its second printing. His criticism of General Lee's staff during the campaign, particularly in the case of Colonel Marshall, was uppermost in his mind.

Sept. 13th 1908   Department of Justice
                                                   Washington

Dear Sam:

I suppose, as you wrote me, you will leave tomorrow for Lynchburg Court. I wrote Nonnie Cosby that you were coming & that they must take good care of you. I suppose you will go to Bedford & spend a Sunday with Willie.[1] You are always welcome there & are a great favorite of many. The *Times-Dispatch* of next Sunday will have a letter of mine in which I expose the "true inwardness" of Gen. Lee's Staff Officers. Tell Hugh; also Stockton Terry. Give a copy of it to Judge McDowell.[2] If you see Miss McDowell tell her to give my love to her mother. I remember her as one of the handsomest girls I ever saw. You will probably see John Daniel in Lynchburg. I met him here on the day he returned from Europe. He said he would make some speeches for Bryan.[3] John[4] will speak (nominally) for Bryan—really for John—but will pray (like Joe Bryan) for Taft's election. I went to Warrenton last Monday to register as I want to vote for Taft.[5] I have been looking for the Rev. [illegible—may be J. Wise] to pick on me—or my book. I have a letter from Major Swift of the Army War College saying that he is preparing a review of my book for the Journal of the United States Cavalry Association wch. ought to give it a good send off. The truth is I wrote the book for soldiers and students of military history. I think it will have great value.

Yours Truly
Jno. S. Mosby[6]

Senator John Daniel's home was in Lynchburg. Stockton Terry had been living in Lynchburg since the end of the war.

1. Colonel Mosby's brother, Willie, lived in Bedford, Virginia.
2. Judge Henry Clay McDowell was a lawyer and a U.S. judge for the Western District of Virginia. He was also a friend in good standing of Colonel Mosby.
3. William Jennings Bryan, Democratic nominee for president.
4. John Daniel, incumbent senator from Virginia.
5. William Howard Taft ran for president against the Democrat William Jennings Bryan.
6. GLC 3921.24. John Mosby. Autograph letter signed: to Sam Chapman, 13 September 1908 (The Gilder Lehrman Collection, courtesy of The Gilder Lehrman Institute of American History, New York).

Scenes from the Past

Colonel Mosby wrote to Sam Chapman the day following his previous letter. In this short note he was nostalgic about Bristol, where he had his law office just prior to the war, and nearby Abingdon, Virginia, the county seat where he enlisted.

September 14th 1908   Department of Justice
                                       Washington

Dear Sam:

Herewith I send a copy of a letter from Major Swift, the Director of the War College. His review should give my book a good send off. It was really written for military students. I suppose you will arrive in Lynchburg this evening. Be sure to go to Bedford. I hope to be well in November & pay a visit to Bedford & go on to see my old home in Bristol. Of course I shall stop at Abingdon & see the old camp ground where I first stood guard & called for the countersign. Remember me to Stockton & give my love to the Cosbys.

Yours Truly,
Jno. S. Mosby[1]

I wrote you yesterday that the *Richmond Times-Dispatch* next Sunday will have a letter of mine. Tell Stockton I want him to read it.

---

1. Stuart-Mosby Historical Society Collection.

"There Is No Future for Me"

John Mosby received and wrote much correspondence relative to his book on the Gettysburg campaign. One of his grandsons, Spottswood Campbell, graduated with a law degree and then practiced in New York. Still, the aging veteran brooded. Though he did not mention it in this letter to Chapman, a primary reason for his sadness was the death of his close friend Joe Bryan less than a month before.

Dec. 14th 1908   Department of Justice
                                       Washington

Dear Sam:

I shall leave here on the 19th (Saturday) and spend a few days with my relations in Lynchburg—then go to Bedford so as to be there Xmas. Hope you will arrange your visit to Bedford so as to be there when I am there. Did Josie come out for Taft before the election? I have never heard. I see it stated in the Washington papers that the deputy marshals are to be put in the Classified Service. I hope this will be done so that you will be safe if there are any changes. There is no future for me—my course is run [illegible] I don't remember that I wrote you that I got Spottswood Campbell—who graduated in law at the University last June—in the biggest law firm in New York through the influence of Cecil Hubbard who was with Sheridan in the Shenandoah Valley. I told Spottswood that he owed his good fortune to his mother. Please send me a schedule of the steamers—I want to write to Willie.

Yours truly
Jno. S. Mosby[1]

Thanks to the generosity of Joe Bryan, both of Mosby's grandsons, Spottswood and Mosby Campbell,[2] were able to graduate from the University of Virginia and begin their careers. In writing to Mosby concerning the education of his grandsons, Bryan said: "I want to be your partner in this business."[3] Now Joe Bryan was gone and Mosby was heartsick. In a letter to a friend shortly after Bryan's death, Mosby confided: "I returned to Washington last Sunday evening because I could not bear to be in Richmond after Joe Bryan had gone. He was the best friend I had in this world; I never expect to see his like again."[4]

1. Peter A. Brown Collection (previously transcribed copy).
2. Sons of Mosby's late daughter, May, who had married Robert Campbell, also deceased.
3. Siepel, *Rebel*, 274–75.
4. Mitchell, *Letters*, 155; John Mosby to Thomas Nelson Page, November 28, 1908.

Lincoln, Slavery, Secession

John Mosby was caught up in the old slavery-secession argument again in this letter to Sam. A magazine article appeared to have brought the matter to the fore.

Feby. 10th 1909   Department of Justice
                                   Washington

Dear Sam:

I want you to read Watterson's article on Lincoln in the
March *Cosmopolitan* Life of Judah Benjamin.[1] Then ask
Hugh[2] how much worse it was for Lincoln to set the Negroes
free than for Jeff Davis to have done it. I suppose Gordon[3] can
give some metaphorical distinction; I can't.

Yours truly,
Jno. S. Mosby[4]

Did you read in *The New Republican* paper at Staunton last
week an extract from Alex. Stephens speech against secession
in which he predicted the war would follow it?

In what came to be known as the Hampton Roads Conference, President Lincoln and Secretary of State Seward met with Confederate Vice
President A. H. Stephens and two other representatives of the Confederacy, Robert M. T. Hunter and John A. Campbell. Supposedly,
Lincoln made an offer of compensation for all the freed slaves—to
the extent that he was able to promote it—but in the end the talks
failed. The Confederacy insisted on independence, the North on rees-
tablishment of the Union. Alexander Stephens, speaking as a member
of the Georgia legislature against secession, in February 1861 said:
"We shall be in one of the bloodiest civil wars that history has ever
recorded."

1. Coulter, *A History of the South*, Vol. 7; the Confederacy's first attorney
general and later secretary of state.
2. Hugh McIlhany.
3. Armistead Gordon.
4. GLC 3821.25. John Mosby. Autograph letter signed: to Sam Chapman, 10 February 1909 (The Gilder Lehrman Collection, courtesy of The
Gilder Lehrman Institute of American History, New York).

Trying to Get a Judge "Promoted"

John Mosby put on his political hat in the first postwar election for a Virginia governor when he introduced Gilbert C. Walker to a Warrenton audience in the summer of 1869;[1] afterward he would rarely take it off. Four decades later, he was trying to gain a federal judgeship for his friend Henry Clay McDowell, and he asked Sam Chapman to do some of the legwork.

March 9th 1909   Department of Justice
                                                 Washington

Dear Sam:

I suppose you are now in Lynchburg. I want you to see Judge McDowell about his getting promoted to the Supreme Court. Taft will have several appointments as three or four judges must retire on account of age. The South has no representative there & I really don't know any Southern Republicans fit for the position except Judge McDowell. Mr. Taft must appoint either a Democrat or McDowell. I have a strong desire for his appointment (1) because his home is in Virginia & (2) because he is a grandson of Henry Clay. I dined Saturday with Col. Charles Francis Adams. He is spending the winter here with his family. He was in Virginia during the war—commanded the First Massachusetts Cavalry. Give my best to Stockton & my cousins.

                                                 Yours Truly
                                                 Jno. S. Mosby[2]

Does Hugh stand by the Confederate daughters in the decoration of graves?

Judge McDowell failed to get the appointment.

1. Siepel, *Rebel*, 173–74.
2. GLC 3921.26. John Mosby. Autograph letter signed: to Sam Chapman, 9 March 1909 (The Gilder Lehrman Collection, courtesy of The Gilder Lehrman Institute of American History, New York).

The "Trial" of Jefferson Davis

Colonel Mosby visited the University of Virginia to say good-bye to the daughter of a former member of his command, John McCue. He discussed an incident involving the girl's father and General Grant during the war. He also replayed his thoughts on the Jefferson Davis non-trial.

———

June 18th 1909   Department of Justice
                                 Washington

Dear Sam:

We returned yesterday from the University[1]—had a nice time. I suppose you read my letter in the *Times-Dispatch*.[2] In yesterday's paper is a letter from as great an Ass as J. William—he called it an answer to me. Now I want you to get Gordon to read my letter & the answer—so called—and ask him if one thing I stated has been controverted. He said that on a demurrer to the indictment for treason Chief Justice Chase had decided that Davis was not guilty of treason. I denied it and said that Chase could never have made such a decision as there never was a demurrer to the indictment and the only question before the Court was whether or not Davis had already been punished for treason. Davis' guilt or innocence was never mentioned. Now that is the way they make history in Virginia. Virginian's have [illegible] theology as much as Greeks and Romans. You know I am always ready to help you whenever I can.

The University is on a boom—just raked in over a million of Yankee money and poor professors retired and living [illegible] on the Carnegie Foundation—but like Oliver Twist they are calling for more. I called again at the University to say good-by to John McCues's daughter. This is the kind of reunion I like. You know Grant went to the White House with John's mother and told Andy Johnson, who had refused him a pardon, that he would not leave the room until he signed the boy's pardon. This was the same Andy for whom the Virginia delegation voted for President in the Democratic National Convention in 1874–75. Dr. Alderman promised to invite Taft and Fred Grant[3] to the University on next Founder's Day (April 13th). I have a very nice letter from Fred. I wrote to him how pleased I was in the grand ovation the old Confederates gave him at Memphis. It was both a tribute to his father & vindication of me for supporting him. "Hence time at last makes all things even," Byron says in Mazeppa.[4] I was only 40 years ahead of the times—Ask Hugh.

Yours truly
Jno. S. Mosby[5]

———❦———

John McCue was an eighteen-year-old V.M.I. cadet when he enlisted in Mosby's command in 1864. While with the Chapman brothers in the Northern Neck in March 1865, he and two companions attempted to capture the post office across the Potomac River at Croom, Maryland. McCue was captured after a fire fight in which one man was killed. Although in Confederate uniform, McCue was tried for murder and sentenced to life imprisonment at hard labor. As Mosby related, with the help of General Grant, the boy was pardoned.[6]

1. The University of Virginia.
2. *Richmond Times-Dispatch*, June 15, 1909.
3. Son of General and President U. S. Grant.
4. Byron wrote this poem based on the true story of Mazeppa from Voltaire's "The History of Charles XII, King of Sweden."
5. Hugh Keen Collection (previously transcribed).
6. Brown, *Mosby's Fighting Parson*, 283; Keen and Mewborn, *43rd Battalion*, 346 (roster).

The Virginia Secession Conventions

Colonel Mosby pointed out to Sam some of the people who originally voted against the Ordinance of Secession in Virginia but reversed their stand on the final ballot. Mosby painted one family with his sarcastic brush for securing government jobs following the war.

———❦———

John S. Mosby as a major in 1863. He held this rank for only ten
months before again being promoted.

Sam Chapman was promoted to captain and married the same day, July 28, 1864 (from *Mosby's Rangers*, by James J. Williamson).

Lt. Col. William Chapman, Sam's brother, was second in command of Mosby's battalion (from *The Memoirs of Colonel John S. Mosby*, edited by Charles W. Russell).

Colonel Mosby, shortly after the end of the war; possibly his last picture in uniform (from *The Memoirs of Colonel John S. Mosby*, edited by Charles W. Russell).

William H. "Willie" Mosby, who served in his older brother's command, was a close friend of Sam Chapman (from *The Memoirs of Colonel John S. Mosby*, edited by Charles W. Russell).

Sam and Rebecca Elgin Chapman. From the original tintype, thought
to have been taken on their wedding day, July 28, 1864 (Joe Bauman
family collection, Salt Lake City).

Colonel Mosby was seventy-one years old when he was appointed an assistant attorney general in the U.S. Department of Justice (from a 1904 newspaper).

Rev. Sam Chapman, minister of Covington (Va.) Baptist Church, c. 1882.

William Chapman ("Col. Wm.") in San Francisco after the war.

William A. "Willie" Chapman (Sam's son) lived in San Francisco along with Colonel Mosby, who said of Willie, "I feel towards him as if he were my son" (Charles C. Lewis collection).

Col. William Chapman and Josephine Jeffries were married in February 1864. This picture is believed to have been taken on their fiftieth wedding anniversary. For reasons not known, Colonel Mosby often made disparaging remarks about "Josie" and her mother in letters to Sam Chapman.

Center, Colonel Mosby; left, Lt. Charles Grogan; right, Dr. W. L. Dunn. Mosby's expression possibly reflected his attitude of impatience with the artist, as described in his letters to Sam Chapman.

Above and facing page: *Mosby and His Veterans*, a Mosby tryptych by Otto Walter Beck (John T. Kinchloe collection).

Right, John Russell;
left, Lt. Fountain Beattie;
standing, Lt. Frank Rahm.

Standing, Dr. James Wiltshire;
seated, Maj. A. E. "Dolly"
Richards.

Sgt. Hugh McIlhany, the "Headless Horseman" of Mosby's letters (from *Mosby's Rangers*, by James J. Williamson).

Colonel Mosby at eighty years of age in 1915, the year before his death (from *The Memoirs of Colonel John S. Mosby*, edited by Charles W. Russell).

Department of Justice,
Washington. Dec: 13ᵗʰ /904

The President:

This will introduce a friend—
Captain Sam Chapman—whom
I have known forty years as a
noble, hightoned gentleman.
He has been your earnest
political friend, & deserves
the highest consideration
from you.

Respectfully,
Jno: S. Mosby

John Mosby was an attorney in the Justice Department when he penned this brief note of introduction to President Roosevelt for Sam Chapman. GLC 3921.08. John Mosby. Autograph letter to [Theodore Roosevelt] 13 December 1904 (The Gilder Lehrman Collection, courtesy of The Gilder Lehrman Institute of American History, New York).

Oct. 4th 1909   Department of Justice
                                          Washington

Dear Sam:

Herewith is a letter just rec'd. from Judge McDowell.
Please return it. I sent him a copy of the letter I mailed you
some days ago. You see he says he wants to publish it but I
do not want it published. I don't care however how many you
show it to including Conrad.[1] In the Secession Convention his
father[2] voted against the Ordinance of Secession in company
with John Baldwin, A. H. H. Stuart, & Jubal Early.[3] They
thought there was no cause to justify secession. The court says
there was. Conrad was in the Land Dept. some years ago. (I
suppose he was *forced* in.) His brother Holmes was here in the
Dept. of Justice. I suppose that he was *forced* in. You know
the Court says this is a Government of "*force*" & they have to
submit to it. I sent Col. William a copy.

Ask Hugh if he would not like to be "forced" into office.

Yours truly, Jno. S. Mosby[4]

———————

1. Holmes Conrad Collection, Winchester-Frederick County Historical
Society; Holmes Conrad, son of Robert Young Conrad. He was a lawyer in
his father's law office in Winchester, Virginia, and served in the Virginia Legislature. He also served as an assistant U.S. attorney general and in 1895 was
appointed solicitor general.

2. "Members of the Virginia Convention of 1861," http://members.aol.
com/jweaver300/grayson/1861 conv. Robert Young Conrad, father of Holmes
Conrad and attorney representing Frederick County, Virginia, voted "no" for
secession in the Convention on April 4, 1861; he voted "yes" when the convention met two weeks later.

3. Ibid. In the Secession Convention of 1861, Baldwin and Stuart representing Augusta County, and Early, representing Franklin County, each voted
"no" on April 4 but changed his vote to "yes" on April 17, 1861.

4. GLC 3921.17. John Mosby. Autograph letter signed: to Sam Chapman, 4 October 1909 (The Gilder Lehrman Collection, courtesy of the Gilder
Lehrman Institute of American History, New York).

"I Have Been Avoiding Publicity"

Mosby discussed several things in this letter to Chapman, including actions of Hugh McIlhany's uncle—burning and robbing during the war; Mosby's desire for his friend Judge McDowell to be appointed to a Supreme Court vacancy; and covert operations of the Confederacy.

November 10th 1909   Department of Justice
                                      Washington

Dear Sam:

    Just rec'd. your letter. Instead of seeking I have been avoiding publicity; hence I declined to let my letter to you be published. But I have sent out a number of copies as there are some ideas in it wch. I wanted to be put into circulation. I hope to do some good. Did you read the correspondence & report about burning & robbing cities in *Vols; 43 - Part I & II - Shenandoah Campaign*[1]—You did not mention them. It would be an heroic dose to make Hugh & old Conrad read them. Old Bev Tucker, Hugh's uncle, was engaged in these operations with Clement C. Clay & Jake Thompson. Be sure to read these reports & letters in full. Call on Bowen[2] & remember me to him. My regards to Judge McDowell. Tell him that I want Taft to appoint him to the vacancy on the Supreme Court. I have rec'd. a very nice letter from his wife's mother, Mrs. Clay of Tennessee. I knew her when I lived in Bristol. I wish you wd. write me a long letter. I sent a copy of my letter in reply to the Stonewall Camp to Col. Wm.[3] He showed it to Judge Waddill[4] who was anxious for it to be published.

                                      Very Truly, Jno. S. Mosby[5]

    Clay's letter to Benjamin is anonymous. But see in The Index—Canada—in my letter to Colie Jordan[6] I give the pages & volumes. See also Jake Thompson in Index.

Nathaniel Beverly Tucker,[7] Jacob Thompson,[8] and Clement Clay[9] were all involved in varying degrees with the Confederate clandestine operations out of Canada. Tucker was appointed a deputy Confederate commissioner to procure commissary supplies in Canada. This was his "official" position; he was clandestinely linked with Clay Thompson and others in the Confederacy's Canadian operations. Clement Claiborne Clay entered the Confederate Senate in 1861. He refused an appointment as secretary of war in 1864 but was part of a "peace negotiation" body sent by President Jefferson Davis to Canada to discuss peace with the Union; Lincoln refused their offers and declined to see them. Clay was a veteran of the Southern Army and was sent to Canada in 1864 to try and persuade Copperhead elements in the North to take up arms against the Union. When the war ended and John Wilkes Booth was killed after assassinating Lincoln, the three Confederates, Tucker, Clay, and Thompson, were accused in the conspiracy. Clay turned himself in after a reward was offered for his capture. He was freed after having been imprisoned at Fortress Monroe for almost a year without trial. Thompson fled to Europe and, after years, returned to the United States, later living in Memphis. Tucker, though charged, was never arrested, but was never pardoned before his death in 1890.[10]

1. U.S. War Department, *War of the Rebellion: A Compilation of the Official Records of the Union and Confederate Armies.*

2. Keen and Mewborn, *43rd Battalion* (roster); possibly Frederick Fillison Bowen, who served in Mosby's command; he was a Danville lawyer.

3. Col. William Chapman.

4. Judge Waddill (1855–1931) was a former U.S. congressman from Virginia. He served as judge of the U.S. District Court and in 1908 was appointed to the U.S. Court of Appeals, Fourth Circuit (Virginia).

5. GLC 3921.28 John Mosby. Autograph letter signed: to Sam Chapman, 10 November 1909 (The Gilder Lehrman Collection, courtesy of The Gilder Lehrman Institute of American History, New York).

6. Keen and Mewborn, *43rd Battalion*; Henry Cowles "Coley" Jordan served in Mosby's command.

7. Nathaniel Tucker (1820–1890) served as U.S. consul at Liverpool, England, from 1857 to 1861. (See note 10.)

8. Jacob Thompson (1819–1885) former congressman, served as secretary of the interior from 1857 to 1861.

9. Clement Clay (1816–1882) was twice elected to the U.S. Senate from Alabama.

10. John Headley, *Confederate Operations in Canada and New York*; Tucker, *The Descendants of William Tucker*; Chaitkin, *Lincoln by Anton Chaitkin*; "U.S. Histories, Biographies Encyclope," http://www.allrefer.com.; "Charge and Specifications against [Lincoln Conspirators]," http://www.surratt.org/documents/dcharges.html.

"The Infallibility of Gen. Lee"

Colonel Mosby was unsuccessful in his attempt to obtain a Supreme Court nomination for his friend Judge Henry Clay McDowell, and he urged Sam Chapman to begin a campaign for McDowell's appointment on the U.S. Circuit Court. Rev. Randolph Harrison McKim was scheduled to speak before the Richmond Confederate Veterans' Camp in response to Mosby's recent book defending General Stuart's actions in the Gettysburg campaign. McKim took issue with Mosby's suppositions.

Jany. 21st 1910   Department of Justice
                                     Washington

Dear Sam:

A bill has been passed by the Senate and no doubt will pass the House for an additional U.S. Circuit judge for Virginia. As I like Judge McDowell very much I wd. like to see him promoted from District to Circuit Judge.[1] I think it wd. be well for you to make this suggestion to [illegible] who is a lawyer and he might start a movement in that direction. Do you expect to be here soon? Willie[2] speaks of coming here next week. The *Times-Dispatch* of yesterday has a notice that the Rev. McKim[3] will deliver an address tonight before Lee Camp on "*Stuart's Cavalry in the Gettysburg Campaign* in reply to Col Mosby." It invites the whole world to come and hear The Ecclesiastic. I suppose tomorrow's papers will have a notice of the performance. I sent the *Times-Dispatch* a week ago my reply to Talcott's[4] feeble effort. I had heard from Lawrence Washington[5] who had talked with McKim that his chief point wd. be to show that Gen. Lee's Gettysburg letter to Ewell has

the wrong date. So I anticipated McKim & prove not only
that the date is right but that it wd. have been impossible for
Ewell to have made the movements he did under this order if
the letter had been dated the 29th as McKim contends. The
Chambersburg letter knocks the spy story into a cocked hat
proving it to be a fable. Read Sunday's paper. I have heard
nothing about the Covington P.O. My opinion is that while
Slemp[6] might be pro forma for you for fear of offending
Revercomb;[7] he is really against you as he wants to own all the
office holders in the state. I suppose Hugh will be embarrassed
about taking sides between me and the Priest of his Church.
Tell him I say to take sides with the Truth. The whole trouble I
have is butting up against the popular belief in the infallibility
of Gen. Lee. Hugh's religious Creed is the Trinity & the
infallibility of Gen. Lee. That it is a crime to question the
truth of any statement that has Gen. Lee's name no matter
how absurd his report saying that he ordered Gen. Stuart to
watch Hooker[8] in Va. & inhibit his crossing the Potomac & to
be a hundred miles away at the same time with Ewell on the
Susquehanna. Nobody but a Christian like Hugh can explain
this contradiction. Show him this letter. Remember me to
[illegible]. I had a very pleasant ride with him from Lynchburg
to Bedford. Maybe [illegible] can tell how a man could be on
the Susquehanna and on the Potomac at the same time. I can't.
You know Mahone[9] rode a mule up to heaven one night &
returned before daybreak but nobody but a prophet could do
that.

Yours Truly
Jno. S. Mosby[10]

Reverend McKim's book, *A Soldier's Recollections, A Reply to Col.
John S. Mosby*, disputed Mosby's reasoning in his defense of Stuart.
He delivered a long talk to the United Confederate Veterans in Richmond on the subject of Mosby's book. A major bone of contention
in the argument was the "Chambersburg letter," which contained orders from General Lee to General Stuart. Who actually wrote it and
when? Sam Chapman was still in the U.S. marshal's office in Staunton

but hoped for a possible appointment as postmaster in his hometown of Covington. The postmaster at the time was George Revercomb's brother. Hugh McIlhany was—like Reverend McKim—a member of the Presbyterian faith, and, like most Virginians, was also a great believer in General Lee. Colonel Mosby, although he had high respect for General Lee, believed his first responsibility was to his friend and mentor General Stuart.

1. Judge Henry Clay McDowell was currently setting as U.S. district judge in Lynchburg, Virginia.

2. Willie Mosby, Colonel Mosby's brother.

3. Rev. Randolph Harrison McKim (1842–1920) was a prominent Presbyterian minister and Civil War veteran. His service included that of aide-de-camp, Third Brigade, Johnston Division, ANV, and chaplain in the Second Virginia Cavalry. http://docsouth.unc.edu/mckim.

4. *Richmond Times-Dispatch*, March 7, 1910. Col. T. M. R. Talcott was an aide-de-camp to Gen. R. E. Lee and later colonel of the First Regiment, Engineer Troops, ANV; he wrote a letter to the *Richmond Times-Dispatch* on March 7, 1910, in which he took great exception to Mosby's defense of General Stuart.

5. Probably the father of former Ranger Lloyd Washington of Westmoreland County, Virginia.

6. Campbell Slemp represented Virginia as congressman in the Ninth District.

7. Virginia state senator George Revercomb, brother of Howard Revercomb, and son-in-law of Sam Chapman.

8. Faust, *Encyclopedia of the Civil War*, 369–70. Gen. Joseph Hooker commanded the Army of the Potomac but was relieved three days before the Gettysburg battle; he took command of two Union corps during this time.

9. Woodward, *The Confederacy's Forgotten Son*, 140–41, 151–52, 183. Confederate general William Mahone served gallantly in the Civil War and was a leading player in Virginia politics following the war. The nature of Mosby's reference is not known.

10. GLC 3921.29 John Mosby. Autograph letter signed: to Sam Chapman, 21 January 1910 (The Gilder Lehrman Collection, courtesy of the Gilder Lehrman Institute of American History, New York).

"I Committed Treason & Am Proud of It"

The feud between Colonel Mosby and Reverend McKim continued and Col. T. M. R. Talcott, a former engineering officer with the Confederate Army, had entered the fray. Recalling the campaign for Virginia governor, the first such one held following the war, Mosby defended his actions in not attending a wedding in Upperville with some of the elite of Virginia Conservatives. Mosby talked about why he did not attend reunions of his old command and said he was proud of committing treason.

Feby. 15th 1910   Department of Justice
                                   Washington

Dear Sam:

I suppose you have rec'd. McKim's address—it is in better literary form than Talcott's letter but no better in substance. My answer to Talcott is an answer to McKim. It is not my present intention to publish any answer to him as I have already done that but at my leisure shall write an answer wch. I shall presume you will approve (1) that he takes no notice of the fact that Gen. Lee kept two brigades of cavalry with him; (2) that he never ordered the Army to Gettysburg. He assumes that if Stuart had been with the army Hill wd. not have gone off to Gettysburg. This is a high complement to Stuart. You or I would be glad if somebody wd. say that of us. That wd. not be [illegible] only blame to us if we were off doing our duty somewhere else. Then if Lee never ordered his army to Gettysburg should Stuart be blamed for not being there—any more than you. But see how I have made them back down. The old charge against Stuart was his disobedience to orders— now they say it was only an "error of judgment." You see how Talcott squirms because I said he wasn't mentioned in the reports of the Campaign. He ought not to have put himself up as a target if he didn't want to be shot at. McKim says he rode 50 miles in one day on the campaign. [illegible] an Ecclesiastical lie. There was of course a great prejudice against him. Tyler's wedding (near Upperville) came off the night of that day. I thought my example might do some good—Stayed there & introduced Walker[1] & made a speech. I said that I wd. as soon have videttes to the rear when I ordered my men to charge as to leave Warrenton that day in such a crises when the people of Virginia were standing on the brink. The speech was published in many papers. But the so-called "True Virginians"—Gen. Hunton—Gen. Payne—Col. Tom Smith—Judge (then Justice) Keith—Aleck Payne—all drove off to the wedding before Walker arrived. I was invited to the wedding but wd. not go. But all these men afterward got offices & enjoyed the fruits of a victory wch. they refused to help win. You were there teaching in Warrenton. John Baldwin was examined before the Reconstruction Committee. He was asked if Jeff Davis could be tried before a jury in the South & convicted of Treason. He replied—"yes," that Mr. Davis (& himself) had been guilty of Treason & if they were tried for it now he saw no reason why they should not be convicted. Tell Hugh (for me) that the difference between me & him is that I committed Treason & am proud of it—he committed Treason & is ashamed of it. Baldwin's testimony was in 1867. Dick Smith, in an editorial with the *Enquirer,* was very severe on him. Baldwin replied in a letter. If Sam Yost has files of his paper no doubt you can find it. I am glad to hear that Hugh still has his head on. Ask him who got the price that was set on it. As I have often said I don't go to Reunions because I can't stand the speaking, e.g., Bob Lee's[2] speech at Roanoke about slavery. Why not talk about witch-craft, as he said slavery was not the cause of the war. The articles in the *Sunday Mag.* are a mere synopsis of what I wrote. My kind regards to the "headless horseman"[3] & to Sam Yost.

Yours Truly
Jno. S. Mosby[4]

Charles G. Conner argued Mr. Davis' case. He never mentioned State rights or the right of secession. He contended that the 14th Amendment punished Davis by disfranchisement & was a substitute for the old penalty. Chase agreed & Underwood disagreed with him. Just then the Proclamation of Pardon was issued & Chase ordered the indictment (or case) dismissed because Davis had been pardoned & the pardon put an end to the trial.

Mosby reiterated his belief that slavery was the cause of the Civil War and that, contrary to many opinions, Jefferson Davis was never tried for treason but instead was pardoned.

1. Woodward, *The Confederacy's Forgotten Son*, 141–42; Gilbert C. Walker, a candidate for governor in 1869, was a very conservative New Yorker, put up by the Conservative Party of Virginia. He won the election in a landslide. His administration proved to be one of the worst and most corrupt in Virginia's history.
2. Probably Robert E. Lee Jr.
3. The "headless horseman" who appears so often in Mosby's letters to Sam Chapman seems to be Hugh McIlhany.
4. GLC 3921.30 John Mosby. Autograph letter signed: to Sam Chapman, 15 February 1910 (The Gilder Lehrman Collection, courtesy of the Gilder Lehrman Institute of American History, New York).

Attacking the Dead

A letter from Gen. Henry Heth's brother was published in the newspaper and again brought Colonel Mosby to the firing line in defending General Stuart's actions.

March 21st 1910   Department of Justice
                                   Washington

Dear Sam:

I suppose you have seen the letter of Heth's brother in yesterday's *Times-Dispatch*. Tell Hugh not to be uneasy. I shall take no notice of it. He says Heth did go on July 1st to Gettysburg after shoes. I say that neither A. P. Hill or Heth's reports say they went after shoes. Heth's says he sent Pettigrew[1] on June 30th after shoes, but found out the enemy was holding the place & didn't try to get them. A. P. Hill does not mention shoes. Heth's & Hill's reports say they knew the enemy held Gettysburg but they went to find out how many there were. This was an after-thought to cover up their blunder. They went on a raid but got caught. The first thing I ever wrote about Gettysburg for a newspaper was in December 1877 in reply to an attack on Stuart by Heth. Again in 1891 I said the same about Heth that I say in my book. Again in 1896 Chas. Marshall made his attack on Stuart. I replied & repeated what I had said about Heth. He & Marshall were then living. They made no answer. So it was Heth that first attacked the dead. Now I want you to read in the War Records & ask Mr. Gordon & Hugh to read Heth's & Hill's reports on how they precipitated a battle at Gettysburg & see if I have misrepresented them. Heth's letter written over 30 years ago, wch. Talcott republished, contradicts his report. Heth's brother says that Heth didn't know the Yankees were at Gettysburg. Heth's report says he did know it.

Yours Truly,

Jno. S. Mosby[2]

Col. Charles Marshall was an aide to General Lee, and it was he who usually prepared the first draft of Lee's official accounts of operations of his army. Stuart was slow to make his report to army headquarters of his actions during the Gettysburg campaign, and when he finally handed it to Marshall, an argument ensued in which Marshall was reported to have accused Stuart of disobeying orders. In preparing a draft of the General's report for Lee, Stuart was officially taken to task by Marshall. General Lee refused to adopt Marshall's conclusions with regard to Stuart's actions.[3] General Heth died in 1899, and his brother then made the argument in his defense.

1. Faust, *Encyclopedia of the Civil War,* 179; James Johnson Pettigrew was promoted to brigadier general in 1862 and led a brigade under Gen. Henry Heth. When Heth was wounded in the first day's fight at Gettysburg, Pettigrew took command of the division and led it in the action known as "Pickett's Charge" on July 3, 1863.

2. GLC 5470 John S. Mosby. Autograph letter signed: to Sam Chapman, 21 March 1910 (The Gilder Lehrman Collection, courtesy of The Gilder Lehrman Institute of American History, New York).

3. Freeman, *Lee's Lieutenants,* 3:206–7.

"He Killed My Brother"

On the forty-seventh anniversary of the Miskel's Farm fight, by mere happenstance, Colonel Mosby met the sister of a Union officer killed by Mosby's men during that engagement. Mosby advised Sam Chapman that there was no confirmation yet on Chapman's pending appointment as postmaster in Covington, Virginia.

April 1st 1910   Department of Justice
                                          Washington

Dear Sam:

As I write the above I am reminded that it is the anniversary of the fight at Miskel's where the Rev. Sam sent so many souls to Heaven. Yesterday I met a Va. lady who introduced me to a lady with whom she was talking. The one to whom I was introduced remarked to the other—"He killed my brother." I asked her who he was—She replied "Lieutenant Woodbury"—I replied—"Well, I reckon he was trying to kill me—I have several bullet holes the Yankees put in me." Her brother was killed at Miskel's. I phoned yesterday to Martin[1] about you—he replied that you had not been confirmed but there was no opposition. I have written my answer to McKim but shall rewrite & cut it down. His address is about the weakest thing I ever read.

Yours Truly
Jno. S. Mosby[2]

Shall let you know when mine is published.

On April 1, 1863, Mosby's command, including Sam Chapman, defeated a larger force of the First Vermont Cavalry at Miskel's Farm near the Potomac River. The Union losses were nearly one hundred men killed, wounded, and captured. Among the dead was Lt. Charles A. Woodbury. Mosby's losses were four wounded, one mortally.[3]

1. Senator Thomas Staples Martin of Virginia.
2. Horace Mewborn Collection.
3. Williamson, *Mosby's Rangers*, 54–56, 403–4.

"[Walter Taylor Is] a Great Liar"

Colonel Mosby was going to prepare a final letter on the Gettysburg campaign in reply to comments by Col. T. M. R. Talcott. Mosby felt people were tired of reading about Gettysburg. He accused Col. Walter Taylor, former aide to General Lee, of being "a great liar."

———

April 12th 1910   Department of Justice
                                   Washington

Dear Sam:

    I sent you yesterday a letter from Allen Potts to read.
I forgot to ask you to return it. I hope you have been
inaugurated. I shall not publish a reply to Talcott for a month
or so. People are tired of reading about Gettysburg. I have
to write an answer that will be final. The truth is Talcott is a
mere figurehead—Walter Taylor is the real villain. Taylor is not
fighting for Gen. Lee but for himself. I have proved him to be a
great liar. He is trying to prove his innocence at the expense of
Gen. Lee.

                                   Yours Truly
                                   Jno. S. Mosby[1]

———

Mosby continued to express strong hostility toward General Lee's staff. He took Colonel Taylor, one of Lee's aides-de-camp, to task regarding reports made about the Gettysburg campaign and Stuart's role. Sam Chapman was finally confirmed—"inaugurated"—as the Covington, Virginia, postmaster.[2]

    1. GLC 3921.31 John Mosby. Autograph letter signed: to Sam Chapman, 12 April 1910 (The Gilder Lehrman Collection, courtesy of The Gilder Lehrman Institute of American History, New York).
    2. Brown, *Mosby's Fighting Parson*, 345.

Superannuated

U.S. Attorney General George Wickersham asked Mosby to submit his resignation from the Justice Department, effective July 1, 1910. Mosby's brother-in-law, Assistant Attorney General Charles W. Russell, was assigned to a position out of the country, and Mosby had lost his last anchor in the rough waters of government patronage. Wickersham apparently said that he, Wickersham, hardly knew Russell.

June 20th 1910   806 12th St. Washington

Dear Sam:

Your letter rec'd. You say the Attorney General hardly knew Russell. How did you find that out? I thought he knew him very well. Russell as an Asst. Atty. General was brought into daily contact with him & of course Russell knew him well & he knew Russell. On the contrary, as I was under Russell he kept me under cover & I never met Wickersham here but once—when I called over a year ago for a minute to pay my respects. Who told you that he hardly knew Russell? Nobody can do anything for me; nor do I consider it only stranger that the Administration should want to get rid of me than of anybody else.

Yours Truly
Jno. S. Mosby[1]

Three weeks after writing the above letter Colonel Mosby wrote to an acquaintance in Boston: "No reason was assigned to me for it, but I have heard that the alleged ground for it was that I am superannuated; of which I am unconscious. I believe that I retain all my faculties, mental and physical in as good a condition as they were thirty years ago."[2]

1. GLC 3921.32. John Mosby. Autograph letter signed: to Sam Chapman, 20 June 1910 (The Gilder Lehrman Collection, courtesy of the Gilder Lehrman Institute of American History, New York).
2. Mitchell, *Letters*, 160; John S. Mosby to Col. E. Leroy Sweetser, July 13, 1910.

"I Was Kicked Out"

When John Mosby returned east from San Francisco for good in 1885 he left behind his close friend Willie, son of Sam Chapman. Ensuing correspondence between the crusty old veteran and the young sailor had lessened, much to the distress of Mosby. Willie was still at sea with the shipping company. In this letter to him, Mosby discussed the Forbes family. Following the war Mosby became close friends with this former enemy and his family.

January 22nd 1911   1130 12th St., Washington, D.C.

Dear Willie:

    I haven't had a line from you for over a year. Some months ago I wrote you a letter & enclosed a check for $10 with wch. to buy me some kakis.[1] You must have rec'd. the letter as the check came to the bank with your endorsement but I got no other reply from you. Your father wrote me that you wd. be back early in Feby. from Hong Kong so I enclose this letter to him to forward to you. I got a royal reception in Connecticut. I wish Sam could have been with me. I know he wd. have enjoyed it. By request I have written some articles wch. I want you to read—Two for *Munsey*—one will appear in March—The other in April—and one for *Leslie's Weekly*[2] wch. will appear in April. Do you ever see or hear of the Forbes'? Does Katy still go with the Salvation Army? How is our friend Bowman & the Casta Blanca. I enclose you my card of introduction to Cameron Forbes of the Philippines. He is the son of Major Forbes whom we captured. His family have been my warm friends ever since the War. I recently had a letter from his sister, Edith, the wife of Prof. Webster of Harvard. His mother—a widow—is the daughter of Ralph Waldo Emerson.[3] Two years ago I called on Cameron Forbes at the New Willard—he was out—I left my card. Then he called on me & I was out. You have heard of course that I was kicked out of the Dept. of Justice. I am still living the Connecticut people say! Please find out if my old friend Von Duzen is living

& his address. Remember me to Miss Kidder.

Yours Truly

Jno. S. Mosby (over)[4]

Just before I went to Hong Kong your father and I dined at The Arlington with Major Wm. H. Forbes[5] (whom we captured—the father of Cameron.) One of my men took Maj. Forbes' watch when he was a prisoner. Your father took it from the man & gave it back to Forbes. After I returned from Hong Kong Forbes gave me a banquet in Boston. One of his sons was there. I suppose it was Cameron.[6] Then I met Mrs. Forbes, her daughter Edith, & one of her sons at the Palace Hotel in 1900 & dined twice with them.

The Forbes family, with whom Colonel Mosby established a close friendship after the war, was a prominent one in New England. Major Forbes's father, John Murray Forbes, made a fortune in the railroads in the middle-to-late nineteenth century. Major Forbes risked the family's fortune to financially back Alexander Graham Bell's fledgling telephone company and became the firm's first president. Colonel Mosby's article, "Personal Recollections of General Lee," in the April 1911 issue of *Munsey's Magazine* related the remarkable, yet questionable ill feelings that supposedly prevailed between Lee and Gen. George E. Pickett, of Gettysburg fame. Included in the article was the alleged order that Lee had issued for the arrest of Pickett in the closing days of the war. Mosby's remembrance of Lee's icy snub of Pickett at a Richmond hotel in 1870 was also there. The incidents related by Mosby cast a shadow upon the characters of both Lee and Pickett.[7]

1. An Asian persimmon widely consumed in the Orient.
2. The article in *Leslie's Weekly* appeared on April 16, 1811, entitled "Why I Fought for Virginia." The Colonel went into detail on his prior station in life as a young lawyer and his political views then.
3. The noted abolitionist and poet laureate of New England.
4. Horace Mewborn Collection.
5. Brown, *Mosby's Fighting Parson*, 180–83. Major Forbes and his command, consisting of portions of the Second Massachusetts and Thirteenth New York Cavalries—about 250 men—were attacked by Mosby's Rangers—about 150 men—

near Mt. Zion church on July 6, 1864. The brutal fight resulted in the killing or mortal wounding of over 50 or Forbes's men and the capture of over 100.

6. Cameron Forbes used his wealth as an investment banker to become governor general of the Philippines in 1908.

7. *Richmond Times-Dispatch,* letter from Miss K. C. Stiles, March 21, 1911; letter from Jno. S. Mosby to Eppa Hunton, March 25, 1911; letter from M. G. Elzey, April 2, 1911; letter from Clifford Dowdey, October 5, 1957.

Some Advice on Mail Delivery

John Mosby's younger brother, Willie, was postmaster in Bedford, Virginia. Both Mosbys rendered unsolicited advice to Sam Chapman relative to his operation of the Covington post office.

May 2nd 1911   Bedford City, Va.

Dear Sam:

Your letter rec'd. I spent yesterday at Roanoke—saw Andrew.[1] Willie thinks you ought to have free delivery.[2] from your office—that it wd. relieve you of some of the work you now do—that it wd. of course be far more agreeable to the patrons of the office to have their mail brought to them than to have to go after it themselves & that you are the proper person to apply for it. He had it done here. Then some of your friends wd. get places as mail carriers. Nobody gets anything in this world without asking for it. Urge Hitchcock[3] to give you a free delivery. I return to Washington tomorrow (1130 12th St.) I wish you wd. go there & see Hitchcock—no doubt the patrons wd. sign a petition for free delivery. Revercomb could attend to that for you. My article which the *N. Y. Herald* has accepted will be syndicated—i.e., published on Sundays the same day in a number of newspapers in different places wide apart. I think The *Herald* syndicates with the *Wash. Post.* If so, it will be in both papers in the *Sunday Magazine Section* on the same Sunday. It tells how Fitz Lee saved Pope's army. Hugh will cry when he reads it.

Yours truly, Jno. S. Mosby[4]

1. Andrew Chapman, youngest of Sam's brothers; he lived in Roanoke, Virginia.

2. Colonel Mosby suggested Sam get rural free delivery (RFD) for outlying areas from his post office.

3. Frank H. Hitchcock, the postmaster general.

4. GLC 3922.33. John Mosby. Autograph letter signed: to Sam Chapman, 2 May 1911 (The Gilder Lehrman Collection, courtesy of The Gilder Lehrman Institute of American History, New York).

A Letter to Willie

In this letter to Willie Chapman, Sam's seagoing son, Colonel Mosby acknowledged receipt of the kaki. Mosby had been in Norfolk seeing the sights and wished Sam could have been there with him.

August 26th 1911   1130 12th St., Washington

Dear Willie:

The package of kakis arrived yesterday. I got back the night before. Many thanks. On my trip I made a complete circle. Much to my surprise a bank sent me a check to pay for my expenses on this excursion. It was a contribution from friends. It was stated who they were. All of wch. proves the truth of what I have often said that the world is growing better every day. I hope you can come to see me before you leave. I was kindly treated wherever I went. At Norfolk the Admiral showed me over the [illegible] Louisiana. There I went on a training ship where I met Admiral Reynolds[1] whom I had known in Hong Kong.[2] Then to the great winery. The proprietor sent a case of his wine to Ocean City for me. Of course a lot of the pretty girls showed their affections for me & I wished that the Reverend Sam had been there to enjoy the distribution of favors—not the kind, however, to send the Reverend Knott.[3] My regards to Sam.

Yours Truly
Jno. S. Mosby[4]

---

1. Arlington National Cemetery Website. Rear Admiral Alfred Reynolds, a native of Hampton, Virginia, graduated from the U.S. Naval Academy in the class of 1873; his appointment as rear admiral was received July 11, 1911. Much of his career was spent on ocean-going vessels. The admiral's son, Bainbridge, was a midshipman at the Naval Academy.

2. Mosby served as U.S. consul in Hong Kong, 1879–1885.

3. Knott's identity is unknown. A possibility is Richard Knott, a private in Mosby's command; his service record is quite limited and his postwar life unknown.

4. (Copy) Peter A. Brown Collection.

A New Address and Old Clients

Colonel Mosby had moved his residence and took the occasion to look over some old papers.

———

October 30th 1911   1212 12th St., N.W.
                                            Washington

Dear Sam:

Observe my new address—three 12s—same St. & only a few doors from my former. The case for my moving is the death of my landlady. In looking over a lot of old papers I found the enclosed letter from Mr. Ran Tucker[1] written when he was leaving Va. to locate in Baltimore. The persons to whom he alludes were wealthy clients of mine in Baltimore & to whom I had spoken about employing him with me. I suppose Mr. Henry St. George Tucker[2] wd. like to have this letter as a memento of his father & you can send it to him.

Yours truly
Jno. S. Mosby[3]

———

1. John Randolph "Ran" Tucker was a six-term Virginia congressman and former professor of law at Washington & Lee University.

2. Henry George Tucker, congressman from Virginia, was professor at W&L University and George Washington University. Son of the late Ran Tucker, he also served six terms in Congress.

3. GLC 3921.35. John Mosby. Autograph letter signed: to Sam Chapman, 30 October 1911 (The Gilder Lehrman Collection, courtesy of The Gilder Lehrman Institute of American History, New York).

"Old Joe Was Really Retreating"

Colonel Mosby again moved his residence within the city but did not spend time "decorating." He had been traveling—to Richmond, Petersburg, and Baltimore—and was back in Washington but planning a trip to Bedford, where his brother, Willie, lived. He had also just written to Sam's son Willie.

———◆———

May 30th 1912   136 East Capitol St., Washington

Dear Sam:

I am not engaged in decorating. I am spending the day writing letters; have just mailed one to Willie[1] who is due in S. F. next week. I had a very pleasant time in Richmond—went over to Petersburg & spent a night with Stith Bolling. Also went last Friday to Baltimore as I had not seen Pauline & Ada[2] since last Xmas. The way in which Teddy has knocked out Taft is one of the most surprising phenomena of history. I never could believe that Teddy would be a candidate until he actually announced himself.[3] In Baltimore I called on the Cardinal & Mrs. Bonaparte.[4] We made no allusions to politics except that Bonaparte (who is my friend) announced that it might be better for me if he were in the Dept. of Justice. Still I am not for Teddy's nomination—hope it may all result in the nomination of Hughes[5] or Root.[6] I suppose you have seen the June *Munsey* with a piece on Stonewall Jackson. There is a printer's error on the third line of the heading—Byron wrote (siege of Corinth) "would" the printer put "could." Near the end I wrote "has been," the printer put "had." I wrote Bonaparte—printer put "Napoleon." Some of the best things in my Msc. are omitted in both *Munsey & Leslie*. Speaking of my being shot when a prisoner I said that several claimed credit for it & that in reply to one who wrote to me I wrote back that if I had ever been guilty of such an act I wd. not admit it & that it could never have been proved by me. It is edited so as to make nonsense—"he" is inserted for "I". Still I think my article on Jackson presents a view of the First Bull

Run Campaign that is new—i.e., that Johnston retreated from Harper's Ferry & that as Jackson left Winchester at noon on the 18th when the fight was going on at Blackburn's Ford Johnston could not reasonably have expected his troops to reach there in time to reinforce Beauregard. Old Joe was really retreating. I shall go to Bedford on August 1st—Stop on the way at Massanutten Springs.

Yours Truly

Jno. S. Mosby (over)[7]

I omitted to enclose the card to Willie in the letter just mailed to him. Please send it to him. It may be to his advantage to present it. There is a U.S. Cavalry Camp in the Philippines named "John S. Mosby."

<hr />

1. Willie Chapman.

2. Daughters of John Mosby.

3. Teddy Roosevelt had come out of retirement to form the Bull Moose Party; he out-polled Taft but lost the election to Woodrow Wilson.

4. Charles J. "Cardinal" Bonaparte was former secretary of the Navy (1905–1906) and U.S. attorney general (1906–1909) under President Theodore Roosevelt. In 1908 Bonaparte established the Bureau of Investigation, later to become the Federal Bureau of Investigation. http://www.fbi.gov/fbihistory.htm.

5. Charles Evans Hughes, associate justice of the Supreme Court; he did not run in this election but four years later was the Republican standard bearer, losing to the Democratic incumbent, Woodrow Wilson.

6. Elihu Root, secretary of war under McKinley and Teddy Roosevelt's secretary of state; served as U.S. senator from New York. He had no apparent designs on the White House.

7. GLC 3291.36. John Mosby. Autograph letter signed: to Sam Chapman, 30 May 1912 (The Gilder Lehrman Collection, courtesy of The Gilder Lehrman Institute of American History, New York).

"How Will Josie Vote?"

This short letter was written to Sam Chapman by Mosby from the hospital where he had been a patient for the past week. He was apparently suffering from a recurring bladder problem. However, his desire to vote in the upcoming presidential election was probably a plus in his will to recover. His vote would be against Roosevelt—not necessarily for Taft.

———

Oct. 1912   Garfield Hospital
                                              Washington

Dear Sam:

I came here a week ago today. Don't know how long I shall stay—maybe two weeks or longer. I want to be well when I leave the hospital. Hope to get out in time to go to Warrenton as I did 4 years ago & vote for Taft & against the Bull Moose. Of course, Wilson will be elected. I am glad to see that in a letter he came out in favor of putting all offices in the Classified Service wch. makes you safe. How will Josie vote?
                                    Yours Truly
                                    Jno. S. Mosby[1]

———

Theodore Roosevelt, once one of Mosby's close political allies, made a bid for another presidential term following his hand-picking of William Howard Taft to succeed him four years earlier. His relationship with Taft had cooled, and when he failed to garner enough votes to be the Republican nominee, Roosevelt formed his Bull Moose Party and turned the campaign for the presidency into a three-way horse race. Sam Chapman's position as postmaster was one of political patronage and, unlike those falling under the purview of civil or classified service, was subject to the whims of political preferences. Mosby took another condescending jab at Sam's brother William, and in Mosby's view, Colonel William's domineering wife, Josie. The implication was clear: William would vote how Josie wished, since Josie herself had no vote—suffrage was eight years away.

1. GLC 3921.38. John Mosby. Autograph letter signed: to Sam Chapman, October 1912 (The Gilder Lehrman Collection, courtesy of The Gilder Lehrman Institute of American History, New York).

A Kiss from Lady Astor

Colonel Mosby was visited by the future Lady Astor. Though still in
the hospital, he made plans to go to Warrenton to vote.

———⊶⊷———

Oct. 29th 1912   Garfield Hospital

Dear Sam:

Your letter just rec'd. I return you the $5.00 enclosed. I do
not need it. Fount was here yesterday. He agreed to go with
me to Warrenton next Sunday. I do not like to travel alone.
I shall vote for Taft, return on same day to Washington. If
Wilson is elected as I am sure he will be, it will be far better
for the country that his election is overwhelming—then he will
be less partisan and & the Bull Moose will be buried forever.
His academic training should make him in favor of a cleansing
of the classified service. Of course this can be no benefit to
me but will be to you. A few days ago I got a letter from Ms.
Waldorf Astor[1] inviting me to visit at her father's home—
Mirador—in Albemarle.[2] I replied that it was impossible—I
was in a hospital. Then she wrote me that on her way home to
England this week she would stop by to see me. Yesterday she
came with her sister. It was a coincidence that as she walked
in my room a nurse followed her with a magnificent bouquet
& a card with the inscription "Compliments of the grandson
of your friend." Signed Capt. U. S. Grant, 3rd. Of course
it was gratifying to be this remembered. On my table were
two large photos taken in Bristol. I told Ms. Astor that I was
saving them, for her to take her choice. The other was for my
granddaughter. When they left both leaned over the bed and
I kissed their pretty cheeks. Then the sister said "—you ought
to give me that other photo." "Well" I said "you can have it
if you will give me one more kiss." So she came over again &
I gave her another kiss. But to compensate little Pauline[3] for
the loss of the picture she gave me a large red apple grown at
Mirador. You can submit all this to Hugh to determine any
[?] of morality. I think it made me a better man. I promised

Ms. Astor to write my grandson, Spottswood, to call on her at the Waldorf Astoria wch. I did. I also wrote Jack Russell to go & asked them to go off with her to the steam ship next Saturday when she sails for her home in England. Her interest in me may possibly help them. I wrote this to amuse you—but I know it will gratify you to know that I have not forgotten, especially as you did so much to make possible any expectation I had in the War. I hear nothing from Col. Wm. You know that four years ago I had an operation performed. The trouble now is that my bladder has become inflamed. But I am nearly well. My sister Blakely & nephew Hal came to see me today. I don't think you ought to have the slightest fear of losing your place. But I am like Macbeth—"neither foreign envy or domestic malice can hurt me now."

Yours truly,
Jno. S. Mosby[4]

---

1. Nancy Langhorne Astor, formerly of Lynchburg, was married to Waldorf Astor; she became the first woman to serve in England's House of Commons.

2. The Langhorne home, Mirador, is located in western Albemarle County, not far from Charlottesville.

3. Daughter of Virginia Stuart (Mosby) Coleman.

4. GLC 3921.37. John Mosby. Autograph letter signed: to Sam Chapman, 29 October 1912 (The Gilder Lehrman Collection, courtesy of The Gilder Lehrman Institute of American History, New York).

"A Free Trip to . . . Gettysburg"

The fiftieth anniversary of the Battle of Gettysburg was three weeks away, and Mosby was encouraging Sam Chapman to make the trip.

June 12th 1913   The Alamo

Dear Sam:

I recd. a letter from Dolly Richards[1] today saying that he wd. start between July 5th & 10th. I believe they are giving a free trip to old Confederates to Gettysburg. Now Fount[2] & I leave for Elkton[3] next Sunday afternoon—due there at 9:15 P.M. You might go free to Gettysburg & return direct on the N&W[4] to Elkton & you can bring me a great deal of news & learn a good deal. I wish you wd. go. I hear the Elkton Lithia Spring was highly spoken of as well as the hotel there. I do not think that it can be 10 miles from the Massanutten. If the Elkton water does me much good I may stay there a month then go to the Massanutten. I think Willie[5] will stop at Elkton both going & coming from Gettysburg. Josie[6] & Hettie[7] called to see Stuart[8] some days ago. I stopped at the clothing store to see Brooke,[9] where he was the last time I saw him. I was told that he had left there 6 months ago & was preaching around Anacostia.[10] I think he is a bad egg. I do not expect to return here before 15th of August & hope to be so invigorated that I can keep close at work on my memoirs. While at Elkton I want to go to Waynesboro & study up on Jubal's last affair of his Valley Campaign.[11]

Yours Truly

Jno. S. Mosby[12]

Did you ever find Ran Tucker's letter I sent you?

Mosby suffered from a "skin problem" and found the springs soothing to his affliction.[13] Sam Chapman traveled to Gettysburg along with Dr. Will Dunn, a physician who served with Mosby and who had been in private practice since the end of the war. The three traveled in Willie Mosby's automobile. The trip apparently was not without its problems. Willie wrote to Sam a couple of weeks after their return: "I am much afraid that you found me on my Gettysburg trip very irritable and cross, but the truth of the matter is that the boy who drove our machine kept me so infernally mad and irritated that I was hardly myself. I am very nervous and can't control myself as I once could."[14] Willie Mosby died suddenly two months after the return from Gettysburg.[15] He was sixty-seven years old.

    1. Dolly Richards, who became a Kentucky judge, was third in command of Mosby's Rangers in the war.

2. Fountain Beattie.

3. Elkton, Virginia, in the mountains east of Harrisonburg.

4. Norfolk and Western (Railroad).

5. Willie Mosby, John's brother.

6. Col. William Chapman's wife.

7. Josie and William Chapman's daughter.

8. Virginia Stuart (Mosby) Coleman, daughter of John Mosby.

9. Not known.

10. Area in southeast Washington, D.C.

11. Gen. Jubal A. Early and his Army of the Valley fought their last Civil War battle at Waynesboro, Virginia, in the upper Shenandoah Valley in March 1865, one month before Lee's surrender at Appomattox Court House.

12. GLC 3921.40. John Mosby. Autograph letter signed: to Sam Chapman, 12 June 1912 (The Gilder Lehrman Collection, courtesy of The Gilder Lehrman Institute of American History, New York).

13. Mitchell, *Letters*, 186. Mosby made frequent visits to the numerous spas and springs in western Virginia and eastern West Virginia.

14. (Copy) John Singleton Mosby Foundation, W. H. Mosby to Sam Chapman, July 25, 1913.

15. Commonwealth of Virginia, *Death Records of County of Bedford*; William H. Mosby died from "cardiac Depression from overdose of [illegible]." This could possibly be laudanum, a solution of opium in alcohol. This mixture was used in earlier days for pain relief and as a depressant.

"A Very Pleasant Time in Warrenton"

Colonel Mosby returned from a trip to Warrenton, where he cast his vote in the Virginia gubernatorial race. He would soon leave for Baltimore to see his two daughters, Pauline and Ada.

———

Nov. 9th 1913   The Alamo, Washington

Dear Sam:

I went to Warrenton last Tuesday & returned yesterday. Of course I voted for Henry Stuart.[1] I saw Fount last Monday—he said that he intended to vote for Stuart and get even with him. I have no doubt he did. I spent a very pleasant time in Warrenton & was cordially treated. Mrs. Julie Keith[2] came for me in her automobile & took me out to spend the night at Clifton. It is the old Payne Estate just west of the View Tree Mountain. She had a very agreeable company to meet me. I am going over to Baltimore Tuesday to see Pauline & Ada.[3] Found a letter here from my friend Mrs. Astor of London.[4] She is now at her sister's home, Mirador, near Greenwood in Albemarle. I do not remember having told a soul that when I was in the hospital just at this time last year she sent me a check for $500. The world is certainly growing better every day. I hear that Colonel William was in Washington this week. I made Stuart[5] phone yesterday to his daughter but she replied that he had gone to Josie.[6]

Very truly, Jno. S. Mosby[7]

1. Nephew of Gen. J. E. B. Stuart; won the election for Virginia governor in 1913. Mosby was displeased with Henry Stuart for not defending his uncle from criticism relative to the Gettysburg campaign.

2. Member of the family of Judge James Keith, Mosby's former law partner in Warrenton.

3. Daughters of Colonel Mosby.

4. Nancy Langhorne Astor, formerly of Lynchburg, was married to Waldorf Astor; she became the first woman to serve in England's House of Commons.

5. Virginia Stuart (Mosby) Coleman, Colonel Mosby's daughter.

6. Col. William Chapman's wife.

7. GLC 392.41. John Mosby. Autograph letter signed: to Sam Chapman, 9 November 1913 (The Gilder Lehrman Collection, Courtesy of The Gilder Lehrman Institute of American History, New York).

"[Henry Stuart] Is Now Frightened"

Colonel Mosby recalled the time he was wounded by a shot from the gun of a Union cavalryman. He believed that Virginia governor Henry Stuart would be on the next presidential ticket with Woodrow Wilson. Mosby continued to get requests to lecture on his book about General Stuart and the Gettysburg campaign.

Dec. 23rd 1913   The Alamo, Washington

Dear Sam:

Just at this time 49 years ago I was lying at Aquilla Glascock's house suffering from the wound I got at Lud

Lake's & the surgical operation afterward. I have written
Dolly Richards that you wd. probably be here to spend Xmas
& asked him to come if he could. Henry Stuart is here—he
phoned my daughter Stuart today that he wd. call on us soon.
I can never think of him as I once did—(1) his refusal to
endorse a man with such a record as Forrest[1] has as a citizen—
a soldier—& as an official, (2) neither he nor his family has
ever mentioned my book to me although both Henry Stuart
& his father wrote several times to me when I was in San
Francisco asking me to write it. He is now frightened & afraid
he will be held responsible for my articles on Gen'l. Lee's
report. I think it highly probable that Henry Stuart will be
on the next Presidential ticket with Woodrow Wilson & so I
wrote to Dolly Richards whose letter I enclose. I have a letter
from a Military Club in Toronto, Canada asking what I wd.
charge them to deliver a lecture there on *Stuart's Cavalry in
the Gettysburg Campaign*. They evidently have read my book.
I replied $200 & traveling expenses. Have a similar request
from Vermont.

Very truly

Jno. S. Mosby[2]

Mosby received his severest wound of the Civil War on December
21, 1864, when a bullet from the gun of a Union Cavalryman went
through a window pane and struck him in the abdomen. Ludwell Lake
and his family were able to put Mosby, suffering from loss of blood
and indescribable pain, in an ox-cart. They transported him, wrapped
in quilt and blankets and covered with snow and ice, to a nearby house
where Dr. Will Dunn of Mosby's command removed the bullet. Mosby
believed he was dying, as he later wrote to Sam Chapman: "Shortly I
became sick and faint. My own belief was that the wound was mortal; that the bullet was in me; that the intestines had been cut."[3] A
short time later he was recuperating at his parents' home in Amherst
County. Regarding Henry Stuart, Sam Chapman had written a letter
to Mosby: "I was much pleased with your letter to Henry Stuart. He
must be of different metal [*sic*] from his great kinsman. The older I get
the less I like 'jelly fish' people. I meet every day people of more abil-

ity & learning than I have and yet of so little moral courage that I do not care to stay with them."[4] Henry Stuart was not on the ticket with Woodrow Wilson in 1916.

1. Gen. Nathan Bedford Forrest (1821–1877) of Tennessee.
2. (Copy) Peter A. Brown Collection.
3. Brown, *Mosby's Fighting Parson*, 268–69.
4. Duke University, Mosby Papers, Sam Chapman to John Mosby, July 23, 1913.

"A Cat Fight" over Sam's P.O.

Colonel Mosby made final plans for his lecture trip to Toronto. He also was thinking of Sam Chapman's postmaster appointment, which came up for renewal—or not—when his four-year term ended that month. It was truly a patronage position, and with the Democrats in office—both in the White House and in the Senate seats from the Commonwealth—a continued appointment was in doubt.

April 8th 1914   The Alamo, Washington

Dear Sam:

Your letter recd. I am to deliver my lecture at Toronto on the 27th—not before a popular audience but to a Military Institute. People will be admitted by invitation—not by sale of tickets. The day will be Monday. I don't care to get there before Sunday the day before. Have recd. an invitation from a military historian to a dinner on Tuesday afternoon. Frank Pemberton[1] will go with me as I don't like to travel so far alone. I shall leave here about next Wednesday for New York—want to spend some time with my grandsons[2] & Jack Russell.[3] Have finished my lecture—make a great many new points that are not in my book. Don't think my lecture will show any signs of my being superannuated. I have been in hopes that there wd. be a cat fight over your P.O. & that you wd. get the benefit of it. Edw. Borks [?] is still in.

Yours truly, Jno. S. Mosby[4]

Sam Chapman, worried about his postmaster appointment ever since his return from Gettysburg the previous summer, had a postal inspector come to report on his office. Sam wrote to Mosby: "The P.O. Inspector Irving is with me now, checking me up. He told me that he had been ordered to check up this office and report in ten days. He is a right fair man and I believe he likes me. He will find nothing wrong here. I expect Flood or Byrd[5] has been at the Post Office Department arguing the appointment of their man here. I may be removed before the end of my term April 5th, 1914. Well, I shall not cry nor beg."[6]

1. Reader's Digest Assoc., *Family Encyclopedia*. Son of Gen. John C. Pemberton, the "defender of Vicksburg," who surrendered the Mississippi city and 29,000 Confederate troops to Gen. U. S. Grant July 4, 1863.

2. Mosby and Spottswood Campbell.

3. Mosby's nephew, son of his deceased sister Lucie. Jack's father was Charles W. Russell, who married another of Mosby's sisters, Lelia, after the death of Lucie.

4. GLC 3921.42. John Mosby. Autograph letter signed: to Sam Chapman, 8 April 1914 (The Gilder Lehrman Collection, courtesy of The Gilder Lehrman Institute of American History, New York).

5. Heinemann, *Harry Byrd of Virginia*, 4–6; Henry D. "Hal" Flood was a U.S. congressman, and his brother-in-law, Richard Byrd, was in Virginia's House of Delegates; both were Democrats.

6. Duke University, Mosby Papers, Sam Chapman to John Mosby, July 23, 1913.

"Tell [Woodrow Wilson] Who You Are"

Colonel Mosby wrote another letter the next day to Sam Chapman wanting him to go see President Wilson in person. Covington was about fifteen miles from White Sulphur Springs and on the railroad.

April 9th 1914   The Alamo, Washington

Dear Sam:

I have just seen in the *Post* that Woodrow leaves tonight for the White Sulphur to spend his Easter holidays. I suggest you go there & call on him. You need to ask him to keep you on or to put your son-in-law in.[1] But, *incidentally*, you could tell him who you *are* and as well who you *were*. Maybe he will like you so well that he will let you stay in a while longer. I hope at least that he will let the place stay in your family. Well, my lecture is all finished & typed & I am very well satisfied with it. I really don't think it shows any signs of my being superannuated. How is Hugh getting along in his companies? I expect to leave for New York next Wednesday—shall spend about 10 days in the City & at Albany & at Schenectady to see Mosby Campbell.[2] I don't care to get to Toronto before the 26th—Sunday. I deliver my lecture on Monday & am invited to meet a lot of officers at a dinner on Tuesday. I hope the candidates will keep up a fierce fight over your office & keep you in as long as possible.

Yours truly, Jno. S. Mosby[3]

1. Brown, *Mosby's Fighting Parson*, 351; George Stephenson was married to Sam's youngest daughter, Mary, and was an employee of the postal service, but he did not get the postmaster appointment; he was eventually assigned to Richmond as a postal inspector.

2. John Mosby's grandson.

3. GLC 3921.43. John Mosby. Autograph letter signed: to Sam Chapman, 9 April 1914 (The Gilder Lehrman Collection, courtesy of The Gilder Lehrman Institute of American History, New York).

"At War Tomorrow with Mexico"

Colonel Mosby wrote to Sam Chapman from his hotel in New York City, where he was staying on his trip north to Canada. He was still advising Sam, who was not reappointed as postmaster, on what to do in regard to his job-seeking opportunities. Mosby believed war with Mexico was inevitable and forthcoming and Sam might get an appointment in the army as he had in the Cuban conflict nearly sixteen years earlier.

April 19th 1914   Hotel Martinique

Dear Sam:

The indications are that the U.S. will be at war tomorrow with Mexico. Now the thing for you to do is to go to Washington and get the appointment as Chaplain to a regiment. Your experience in Cuba will help you. Go to my friend Judge Watson[1] & show him this letter. He lives at the Cochron. I leave here next Saturday for Toronto—Deliver my lecture on Monday evening—attend a dinner the next day, Tuesday. I presume that I will start back Wednesday night.

Yours truly

Jno. S. Mosby[2]

Mosby's prediction about the United States going to war with Mexico was a little premature. President Woodrow Wilson cautiously watched events unfold south of the border, with the civil unrest there, but no overt action was taken for nearly a year.

1. Judge Walter Allen Watson, former member of the Virginia senate, a circuit court judge, and a U.S. congressman.
2. GLC 3921.43. John Mosby. Autograph letter signed: to Sam Chapman, 19 April 1914 (The Gilder Lehrman Collection, courtesy of The Gilder Lehrman Institute of American History, New York).

"A Conducive Vindication of Stuart"

Colonel Mosby, the international lecturer, was back in New York City following his talk in Toronto. He was extremely upbeat about his reception there, especially by the positive reaction from the military audience regarding his defense of Stuart. His mood allowed him to jest with Sam Chapman regarding the issue of women's suffrage.

May 3rd 1914   Hotel Martinique

Dear Sam:

I returned here two days ago. Shall leave for Washington next Wednesday. I was royally rec'd. by the Canadians & the people of Toronto treated me with great hospitality. My lecture was delivered before the Military Institute & was well rec'd. A vote of Thanks after it was delivered. All the officers thought it was a conducive vindication of Stuart. I have been requested to speak there next Fall. Tomorrow I shall attend a dinner to Forbes-Robertson,[1] the English actor at the Hotel Astor. The cream of N.Y. Society will be there. I am really worn out with dinners & lunches—will be glad to get some repose. Yesterday I got an invitation to a dinner to be given me at Yale on the 4th but was glad of an excuse to decline it as it conflicts with the other dinner. Taft & Cameron Forbes of Boston (son of Major Forbes) were invited. I sent you a marked paper. I found a number in Canada who had read my book. If volunteers are called for I shall ask Woodrow to give me a brigade of suffragettes. They can then enjoy the man's privilege of dying for his country. You have done enough fighting so I want Woodrow to make you my chaplain—you can pray on the suffragettes.

Sincerely,
Jno. S. Mosby[2]

I hope you still hold the fort.

On March 3, 1914, the day before newly elected President Woodrow Wilson's inauguration, a huge parade led by women in support of the Anthony Amendment, which would give the vote to women, started down Pennsylvania Avenue. The peaceful procession soon turned ugly as rioting hostile male spectators broke into its ranks. Troops had to be called in and hundreds of people were hospitalized. Wilson was burned in effigy in other demonstrations led by leaders of the suffrage movement.[3] Thus, Colonel Mosby's tongue-in-cheek comments about the "suffragettes." "I hope you still hold the fort," was a reference to Sam's postmaster position; his appointment term was up but he had not yet received word if he had been reappointed.

1. Sir Johnston Forbes-Robertson, the sixty-one-year-old English actor, was considered the finest "Hamlet" of his time, noted for his elocution and aesthetic features.
2. GLC 3921.45. John Mosby. Autograph letter signed: to Sam Chapman, 3 May 1914 (The Gilder Lehrman Collection, courtesy of The Gilder Lehrman Institute of American History, New York).
3. Reader's Digest Assoc., *Family Encyclopedia*, 1257.

"I Was Splendidly Treated in N.Y."

Colonel Mosby returned to Washington from his long trip to New York and Toronto. He was still on a high from the royal treatment he received in Canada. While he was in New York he received a request from Grand Army of the Republic (GAR) Post in New York to have six of his former Rangers to sit for a group portrait. He told Sam that he, and his brother William, would be included. He asked Sam about his postmaster appointment.

May 11th 1914   The Alamo, Washington

Dear Sam:

I returned here last Monday evening but have not heard a word from you. I am sure that (just as I wrote the last word the post bell rang—I went down—the postman who carries the parcel post had a paper box for me. I opened it—it had a very fine soft (7 1/8—my size) hat for me. It is from Mrs. Halsted of New York, the lady who returned to me my hat that was captured when I was shot at Lake's. This is the second fine hat that has been given to me in the last three weeks.) I wrote & mailed to you & sent you newspapers with accounts of the hospitable reception I recd. at Toronto. They could not have treated the Duke of Connaught—their Governor General—with more attention. The Lafayette G. A. R. Post[1] in New York got me to come & sit for my portrait. They asked me to select six for a group & said the artist wd. come to Washington if they wd. meet him here.[2] Of course you & Fount will be in the group. I have written to Colonel William that he must be one (if Josie consents). A wealthy gentleman—Mr. Benedict[3] called to see me in New York—said that a Society to wch. he belongs wd. like for me to repeat my lecture in N.Y. In October—wch. wd. be a good thing for me. I was splendidly treated in N.Y. Of course Spottswood & Jack Russell shared the kind attention I recd. I am anxious to hear about your post office.[4] So do write to me immediately. The kindness I have recd. goes largely to commensurate me for the loss of office.

Yours truly, Jno. S. Mosby[5]

⸺·⸺

The matter of a group portrait of some of "Mosby's Men" tended to drag for some period of time; eventually it was accomplished but with some changes in the number of men and in those chosen to sit. The old Colonel's feelings for the two Chapman brothers was shown by his choosing them for two of the six portrait subjects.

1. The Grand Army of the Republic (GAR) was the Union equivalent of the United Confederate Veterans (UCV). Both organizations were formed by veterans of the Civil War—the GAR in 1866 and the UCV in 1899.

2. Otto Walter Beck was a sixty-four-year-old artist from Dayton, Ohio.

3. The full identity of Benedict is unknown. He is mentioned in several of Colonel Mosby's letters always as only "Mr. Benedict." When he wrote to Mosby he signed his letters with only "Benedict."

4. Ironically, the very day Mosby penned this letter to Chapman, Sam learned that he would not be reappointed as postmaster.

5. (Copy) Peter A. Brown Collection.

"I Did Not Like Col. William's Letter"

Colonel Mosby received a letter from William Chapman in which Chapman apparently defended the commissioner of the Internal Revenue Service in the dismissing of Fount Beattie from the service. Mosby wrote to Sam Chapman of interference within the halls of government—to both keep and dismiss patronage positions.

⸺·⸺

June 9th 1914   Washington

Dear Sam:

Recd. Your letter. No—I do not expect to be away during the month & hope you will come here. I confess that I did not like Col. William's letter in defense of Osborne[1] for dismissing Fount.[2] As he is very intimate with Osborne & Osborne, as he told me, professes to be very friendly to me, I took it for granted that he had told Osborne all about Fount. Now I really doubt if he called Fount; same to Osborne. He says that if I had asked my friend Major Steadman[3] to use his influence with Osborne to keep Fount in he wd. have done it. I wd. not have asked such a favor of the Administration even for myself—according to a rule of courtesy among Congressmen, one—even in the same State—will not interfere in another's district The appointment of a deputy was Carlin's prerequisite. Sweetser's[4] interference wd. have been resented. Now if Osborne wd. have kept Fount in on my account then Col. Wm. might have told Osborne how pleased I wd. be if he did it. If I had been in Flood's[5] position I wd. have kept you on as an old Confederate without regard to politics—but—I could no more have expected that Flood wd. do it than that he could have commanded my battalion. I did have you appointed under Grant although you had not voted for him; nor did I consider it an act of generosity on my part as I was only paying a small part of the debt owed you. Show this to Revercomb.[6]

Very truly
Jno. S. Mosby[7]

Like Fount Beattie, William Chapman was also an employee of the IRS, having obtained the position in the late 1870s after Colonel Mosby declined it.[8] President Hayes had wanted Mosby to take the job of cleaning out the moonshine element in some of the southern states. Mosby recommended William Chapman for the job. William's several differences with Mosby, particularly the one over Fount Beattie's position, served to make their relationship somewhat strained and not nearly as close as the one he shared with Sam.

1. William H. Osborne became commissioner of the IRS in April 1913. "Tax History Project," http://www.taxhistory.org/Commissioners.htm.

2. Keen and Mewborn, *43rd Battalion*, 295 (roster). Fountain Beattie had nearly forty years service with the IRS when he was dismissed. He was seventy-four-years-old.

3. Mitchell, *Letters*, 191, President Woodrow Wilson to Colonel Mos-

by. Mosby sent a copy of his Gettysburg book to President Wilson through Charles M. Steadman.

    4. Ibid., 166–68. Maj. E. Leroy Sweetser was from an old political family in Boston and one of Mosby's supporters when Mosby was let go from the Justice Deptartment in 1910.

    5. Henry D. "Hal" Flood, Virginia congressman.

    6. Virginia state senator George Revercomb, Sam's son-in-law.

    7. GLC 3921.46. John Mosby. Autograph letter signed: to Sam Chapman, 9 June 1914 (The Gilder Lehrman Collection, courtesy of The Gilder Lehrman Institute of American History, New York).

    8. *Washington Times*, April 28, 1894 [date is difficult to read—may be April 23, 1894].

"The State of Virginia Kept Me Locked Up"

The artist who was to paint the group portrait of some of Mosby's men advised that he would not paint from photographs; he declined to include Mosby's deceased brother but later said he would. He wanted to put Mosby in a painting with the recumbent statue of General Lee. Mosby spoke of his bitterness toward his native state.

———

June 12th 1914   The Alamo, Washington

Dear Sam:

    The artist who painted my portrait for the G. A. R. wants to paint a group of six of my men to go with it. He told me that he wd. not paint from photos but only from life. I asked him if he wd. not make an exception of my brother, William as he was my adjutant. He declined but said I could select six. Afterward, Peter Franklin[1] persuaded him to make the exception of Willie. But in the meantime I had told Col. William that he & you wd. be in the group. But as I shall have Willie in it you & he must draw straws for the privilege. I have no doubt that Josie[2] will make things hard. It is all the same. Peter sent me a letter from the artist saying that he wanted to paint a copy of the recumbent statue of Lee & a group of Confederates with it—including myself. But I wrote to Peter declining that honor as it wd. be in bad taste to put a man of a lower rank as I beside General Lee. I suggested these

names—Longstreet—Stonewall Jackson—A. P. Hill—Ewell—
Stuart—Wade Hampton—these are six—if he has more I think
Jubal Early should be there on account of his prominent &
responsible position. His disasters in the Shenandoah Valley
were the inevitable. In his memoir published a year or so ago
he speaks very charitable of everybody but me. I enjoy the
distinction of being the only Confederate at whom he has his
fling. But that does not in the least affect my judgment of Early
as a soldier & it is only in Early the soldier that the world
takes any interest. I say this in the same spirit that I got up out
of my bed in the hospital & went to Warrenton to vote for
Taft after he had kicked me out of office & turned me out on
the cruel charity of the world. Hope to see you soon. Show this
to Revercomb.

Yours truly, Jno. S. Mosby (over)[3]

I enclose another letter from Peter in reply to my declining to
sit in the Lee group, suggesting the names of men that should
be there. You see that he agrees with me. The artist told me
that he was willing to come to Washington to paint portraits
of the living actors. I wrote to Major Dolly—of course he is
willing to come. The artist said nothing to me about painting
a picture of the recumbent of Lee & a group of Confederates
with it. But as he will have to go to Lexington to see the statue
& he might meet you & Dolly in Staunton. I wrote Peter
that to put me in a group with Lee's Generals wd. make me
look ridiculous—a dwarf by the side of giants—a Lilliputian
looking up at Gulliver. Now I am not affecting humility—I
know perfectly well that the investment of history has given
me precedence over other soldiers of my rank in our war. I
do not say that I deserve it—many deserve it—but I am not
responsible for the opinions of the world. The judgement
of contemporaries are often reversed by posterity. I much
prefer being first in one class to being second in another
class. I am one of the few old men who hasn't one single
grievance to complain of. On the whole as compared with
many others I think the world has been very kind to me in
spite of the fact that the State of Virginia kept me locked up

eleven months in the Albemarle jail—which is all that Virginia ever did for me.

———◆———

If any of Colonel Mosby's detractors thought him pompous, that claim could be laid to rest by the manner in which he declined to have his portrait included with that of General Lee and any of his generals. The unassuming manner in which he reacted to the barbs in Jubal Early's memoirs also supports such an assessment. Mosby's treatment at the hands of Virginia's judiciary left him with a very bitter taste.

1. Former Mosby Ranger, who was working in New York.
2. Col. William Chapman's wife.
3. GLC 3921.47. John Mosby. Autograph letter signed: to Sam Chapman, 12 June 1914 (The Gilder Lehrman Collection, courtesy of The Gilder Lehrman Institute of American History, New York).

Fount Does Not Beg

Colonel Mosby showed his feelings relative to Fount Beattie's dismissal from the IRS. Tentative plans were made for Sam and Willie to visit the Colonel in Washington. Mosby said President Wilson would be teaching school after he lost the next election.

———◆———

July 6th 1914   The Alamo, Washington

Dear Sam:

Your letter recd. Am glad to hear that I am so soon to see Willie. Now come this week if you can. I am going to Manassas on Saturday the 18th to look over the battlefield. I want to notify Fount & Hal[1] when you will be here. I doubt now that Osborne ever knew that Fount was a friend of mine & with our command. Because Fount wd. not condescend to beg to keep his office is no evidence that he was indifferent about staying in. Well, Woodrow will not stay in the White House longer than this term. He may then go back to teaching school. Suppose you & Willie will stop with Miss Nellie—I shall tell her that you are coming.

Yours truly

Jno. S. Mosby[2]

I sent Flood[3] a message that he might have made an exception in your case as you were a Confederate soldier & let you keep your office & that 99 per cent of his constituents wd. have not only approved but appreciated it.

Sam and Willie Chapman were unable to visit Colonel Mosby in Washington on the schedule Mosby suggested. (Unable to change his plans, Mosby elected to go to Chapman's home in Covington to see Willie.)[4] There was quite a bit of conjecture on Mosby's part over whether or not Fount Beattie would have lost his position if only the right people had made the right contacts. He believed, for instance, that Osborne, the IRS commissioner, did not know that Fount was a veteran and one of Mosby's closest friends. Likewise, Sam Chapman may have kept his office if Congressman Flood had been contacted relative to Sam's being a veteran and a close friend of Colonel Mosby, even though Flood was a Democrat. Colonel Mosby was adamant that Woodrow Wilson would not be in office for a second term although he had kept the country out of the war raging in Europe with a policy of neutrality.

1. Willie Mosby's son.
2. GLC 3921.48. John Mosby. Autograph letter signed: to Sam Chapman, 6 July 1914 (The Gilder Lehrman Collection, courtesy of The Gilder Lehrman Institute of American History, New York).
3. U.S. congressman from Virginia, Henry "Hal" Flood.
4. Brown, *Mosby's Fighting Parson*, 351–52.

"Put[ting] a New Face on Bull Run"

Colonel Mosby, together with George Tuberville and Fount Beattie, planned to tour the Manassas battlefield on the anniversary of the first battle. Mosby still longed to see Willie Chapman but could not or would not alter his schedule. He was working on his memoirs but was in no hurry to publish them. That summer he would not go to any of the resorts he had visited in the past, due to a shortage of funds. Col. William Chapman still had not written to him since Mosby disagreed with him on the dismissal of the deputy collectors, like Fount, by the Internal Revenue Service.

July 9th 1914   The Alamo, Washington

Dear Sam:

George Tuberville[1] was to see me yesterday. It is arranged that we leave here for Bull Run on the electric car Sunday morning the 20th of July. His team will meet us at Fairfax C.H. We will spend the night at Manassas with Geo. Round [?] and be there on the anniversary of the battle. I think I will put a new face on Bull Run—but not to the credit of Beauregard.[2] I do not care now to change my plan—hope Fount can go with me. Bull Run has been as much misrepresented as Gettysburg. I certainly want to see Willie & am glad to hear that he is able to build a house for you to live in. I shall not go to any resort this summer. I can not afford the expense & I want to keep at work. I think my trip to Canada did me a great deal of good. I am really in no great hurry to publish my Memoirs because if they appear a year hence they will probably be the last book written by a survivor of the war. I have heard nothing from Col. Wm. since his letter defending Osborne for not keeping Fount in. His defense of Osborne was that deputies were not in the classified civil service. I never said they were. I knew they were not—but also knew that Woodrow had sent a message to Congress saying that no deputy collectors should be removed for their politics. Then he allowed Hart to remove all ten. He might at least have spared the only Confederate soldier among them. But all had to go. Yet I am sorry to say the Colonel thinks it was right to turn them out. He also thinks it is right to keep him in. My love to Willie.

Very truly,
Jno. S. Mosby[3]

When Mosby did not want to change his plans, Sam and Willie Chapman were not able to go to Washington to visit him there. But Mosby wanted to see his dear friends, especially Willie, whom he had not seen in a long time, so he made a visit to Covington later that summer.[4] The house Mosby mentioned, that Willie was to build for Sam, was apparently the farmhouse on a large farm that Willie had purchased at auction three years before; it was some three to four miles from town. Sam owned a house in Covington and was living there with several of his children. Willie remodeled the farmhouse, providing Sam with a room and study.[5] Mosby was upset with William Chapman for his defense of IRS commissioner Osborne for allowing Fount Beattie to be removed from office—even after President Wilson had reportedly said that no men in his position would be removed based on politics. Wilson was a Democrat while Fount had secured his position during a Republican administration. Sam, of course, had also been placed in office during Republican president Taft's term and was not reappointed. However, for whatever reason, William did not lose his office.

1. Keen and Mewborn, *43rd Battalion,* 376 (roster); George Richard Tuberville joined Mosby's command as a teenager and saw much action during the war; he was captured at least twice and wounded. He had been working in Washington, D.C.
2. Mitchell, *Decisive Battles,* 356; Gen. P. G. T. Beauregard was field commander under Gen. Joseph Johnston at First Manassas (Bull Run).
3. Peter A. Brown Collection.
4. Brown, *Mosby's Fighting Parson,* 351.
5. Ibid., 353.

It Sticks in Mosby's Craw

Colonel Mosby was still annoyed, after fifteen years, by Dolly Richards's attack on General Grant. Mosby had always blamed Custer for the Front Royal executions, while Dolly blamed Grant. The setting for the group portraits was still up in the air. Mosby refused to see an author wanting to write about him and the command.

August 22 1914   The Alamo, Washington

Dear Sam:

I sent you a marked paper with an anonymous piece I
wrote but put my initials so that you wd. know who wrote
it. I intended it as a defense of General Grant. You know
Dolly Richards made an attack on him some years ago in
a speech at Front Royal & it is a complete answer to Maj.
Dolly. It was a coincidence that on the morning my piece was
published I got a letter from Dolly. I sent him a marked copy
also for the piece was really a rebuke to him. I can't conceive
how a man with any honorable feelings who belonged to our
command could have any but kind feelings for Grant after the
way he treated us from the close of the war until on his dying
bed he penned a tribute to me—which was really as much a
tribute to my men as personally to me. He came to Virginia
believing that we were outlaws like Quantrill's gang.[1] Dolly's
attack on his memory was a small thing & sticks in my craw.
I see they are now accusing the General of committing all
the outrages that we were charged with. [illegible] The real
reason for Dolly's attack on Grant & defense of Custer was
that Custer was a bitter personal enemy of Grant—also a
Democrat. A full week before Custer was killed I was at the
White House seeing Grant. When I came out of the room an
officer remarked to me that General Grant had treated me in a
very different way from the way he treated Custer a few days
before. He said Custer had come to the White House & sent
in his card to Grant & that Grant refused to see him. The wife
of Custer refers to the incident. I was really glad of the excuse
for writing the piece as it puts Grant as well as our command
in a true light. I sent Hugh[2] a copy. I wish you wd. write to
Hugh tell him that I sent you a copy & ask him if I sent one
to him. I don't suppose Hugh is a very strong Woodrow man
since Woodrow turned him down in the post office matter. I
wish you wd. show my piece to Revercomb (if you havn't lost
it.) I asked Hal to tell Col. William (Josie) that I said you &
he wd. have to draw straws for the picture in the group. Hal[3]
wrote that Colonel Wm. (Josie) said that he supposed he wd.

be out of it "as Sam is Colonel Mosby's favorite." Dolly is itching to sit for this. I wrote him that I had heard that a book about our command had just been published. He is evidently ashamed of it & has made no allusion to it. Donnington of the Congressional Library told me about it. It is by that fellow Bennett Young of Ky. who was concerned in the attempt to burn N.Y. City. He wrote to me over a year ago. I wd. not reply to his letters. He then came to Washington— sent me a request through Dr. Lewis for an interview. I declined. The book has Dolly's picture—the only one—he does not mention you or Josie. Send this letter to Willie before you lose it.

Yours truly, Jno. S. Mosby[4]

The question of just who was responsible for the executions in Front Royal has been a subject for debate through the years. The problem between Mosby and Richards was that Dolly blamed Grant while the Colonel placed responsibility on George Custer. None of the upper echelon commanders—Generals Torbert, Sheridan, Merritt, Custer, nor Colonel Lowell—made any mention of it in their reports although all were present or close by on that day.[5] Mosby was beholden to Grant for bringing to an end the harassment Mosby had suffered from the Union military following the end of the war. The general gave orders for Mosby to be left alone after Mosby's wife visited Grant in Washington. She had first gone to President Johnson, who would not intercede, and then to General Grant, who did.[6] McIlhany failed in an attempt to get the Staunton, Virginia, postmaster position. The book referred to was one that briefly told the story of cavalry commands and the cavalrymen of the Confederacy, entitled *Confederate Wizards of the Saddle*; it had just been published. The part dealing with Mosby's command was written primarily about Dolly Richards, who was third in command under Mosby and William Chapman. Mosby thought Dolly was "evidently ashamed of it" because it dealt primarily with him and not Mosby; "embarrassed" was probably a more descriptive word. The author was Bennett H. Young, a member of the Confederacy's "secret service" operating from Canada. It was Young and others who raided the Vermont town of St. Albans in October 1864. He was also named as one who was planning the burning of New York City during the war.[7] Mosby was also on his friend Sam Chapman, apparently because Sam had lost an earlier letter or enclosure that Mosby sent to him and had wanted returned, hence his comments to "show my piece to Revercomb (if you havn't lost it)" and "send this letter to Willie before you lose it."

1. Faust, *Encyclopedia of the Civil War*, 606–7, William Clarke Quantrill was a notorious gambler, outlaw, and murderer when the war broke out. He took his gang and fought on the side of the Confederacy during the first year before beginning guerrilla operations, which were nothing more than robbery, murder, plundering, and pillaging. Because the reports of his atrocities preceded him he was refused a request for a command under the Partisan Ranger Act.
2. Hugh McIlhany.
3. Hal Mosby, Willie's son and Colonel Mosby's nephew.
4. GLC 3073. John Mosby. Autograph letter signed: to Sam Chapman, 22 August 1914 (The Gilder Lehrman Collection, courtesy of The Gilder Lehrman Institute of American History, New York).
5. Brown, *Mosby's Fighting Parson*, 229, 231–33.
6. Mosby, *Memoirs*, 306–7.
7. "A Brief Biography of Bennett H. Young"; "St. Albans Raid," http://www.wv-zone.com/civilwar; Brown, "Confederates in Vermont."

"The Old County Jail Is My Monument"

Dolly Richards had written two letters to Colonel Mosby and had not mentioned the book *Confederate Wizards of the Saddle* in either missive. Mosby talks at length about the Charlottesville jail.

September 14th 1914   The Alamo, Washington

Dear Sam:

I recd. today the enclosed letter from Major Dolly.
Nearly two months ago I wrote him that an employee at the Congressional Library had told me that they had just recd. a book about our command—had his picture in it. But I did not tell him that the employee said his was the only one. This is the second letter I have recd. from him since I wrote that letter to

him but he has never referred to it from wch. I infer that Dolly is rather ashamed of it. I have recd. a notice of the reunion of our men at Charlottesville on the 24th–25th of Nov. Now if you go write me all about it. You can see there the old jail in wch. I was confined eleven months.[1] Some years ago I saw a recommendation in the Charlottesville paper that there be a monument to me in Charlottesville. I told Tom Duke[2] that it was unnecessary to build a monument to me in Charlottesville & that the old County jail is my monument & that my chief regret is that I could not confer on my prison the immortality that Tasso did on his.[3] You know what Byron says about Tasso's dungeon at Ferrara—"*A poet's wreath shall be thine only crown—A poet's dungeon thy most far renown.*" I hope Willie got a letter I wrote him before he sailed. I suppose Hugh will be there with all his frills on. I am keeping close at work— want to go to New York in November. Sorry he didn't get the Post Office. I suppose Josie will be at Charlottesville.

Very truly, Jno. S. Mosby[4]

Colonel Mosby would still try to get Dolly Richards to comment on the book written about the Forty-third Battalion which focused on Richards and in which Richards alone from Mosby's Rangers was pictured. After more than five decades, the deep-seated bitterness Mosby felt from his incarceration while a student at the University of Virginia came to the fore when he received notice of the reunion of his men to be held in Charlottesville. He did not attend, just as he had refused to attend all previous ones save the first in 1895. Mosby indicated Col. William Chapman would be at the reunion when he said—"I suppose Josie will be at Charlottesville." He was sure Hugh McIlhany would be there, and he gave his regrets that he did not get the postmaster appointment he wanted.

1. Wert, *Mosby's Rangers*, 26–27; Mosby was convicted of shooting and wounding another student while at the University of Virginia in 1853. He was pardoned less than a year after.
2. Judge R. T. W. "Tom" Duke was a retired circuit court judge and lawyer in Charlottesville.

3. Taken from the last verse of Byron's "Lament of Tasso," the story of the poet Torquato Tasso's legendary love for Leonara, sister of Duke Alfonsa and of Tasso's resultant imprisonment for seven years by the Duke.
    4. (Copy) Fauquier Historical Society.

"Life of Dolly"

Colonel Mosby sent a "sketch of the operations" of Bennett H. Young, author of *Confederate Wizards of the Saddle*.

———◆———

Oct. 30th [c. 1914]   Washington

Dear Sam:

Enclosed is a sketch of the operations of Dolly's biographer—Bennett Young who wanted to be my biographer but I wouldn't let him be. If you ever see Dolly tell him that it wd. have ruined Quantrill's operations to have had his biography written by Bennett—his friend. I don't think I could have survived & you & Colonel William ought to be glad he does not mention you in his Life of Dolly.

Yours truly
Jno. S. Mosby[1]

Young's expedition from neutral territory was piratical & he ought to have been treated as a pirate.

———◆———

Colonel Mosby showed disdain for Young for raiding from Canada into the United States and then retreating back into Canada—neutral territory. That together with the fact that Young's chapter in his book dealing with the Forty-third Battalion—Mosby's command—was really a "Life of Dolly" was enough to raise the hackles of the tenacious old partisan.

1. GLC 3921.56. John Mosby. Autograph letter signed: to Sam Chapman, 30 October ca. 1914 (The Gilder Lehrman Collection, courtesy of The Gilder Lehrman Institute of American History, New York).

"They Don't Love Each Other"

Mosby wrote to Sam on the anniversary of his, Mosby's, consulate assignment. The portrait paintings were still an ongoing project, and now there were concerns about who would accompany whom to the artist's studio. Colonel Mosby was still in charge after sixty plus years.

——————

Feby 4th 1915   The Alamo, Washington

Dear Sam:

When I wrote the above date I was reminded that this is the anniversary of the day I took charge of the Hong Kong Consulate—36 years ago. I had a letter from the artist telling me that he will paint you & Col. Wm. in the group wch. I suppose will satisfy Josie. The artist says you all must come to New York to his studio at The LaFayette G. A. R. Post. Col. Wm. writes that he is willing to go—so does Major Dolly, Stockton Terry & Jim Wiltshire. I think it best for you all not to go in a group. I want Fount to go with Colonel William. Fount can stay with his son in New York. It won't do for Dolly & Col. William to go together—they don't love each other. My grandson—Spottswood Campbell, my nephew—Jack Russell—are in New York & will be glad to see you. I am dead against Woodrow's shipping bill. It will be an intervention in form of U.S. money if we buy her ships that are interned—shut up—in ports. The artist has a list of 8 for his group—says he is willing to have some more. So I have asked him to include Ben Palmer & John Russell.[1] I do not expect to go to New York this year.

Yours truly

Jno. S. Mosby[2]

——————

It appeared that the list for the group portraits was set—for now—but appearances could deceive. The artist had consented to have both William and Sam Chapman painted, thus relieving them of having "to draw straws" for the privilege. Colonel Mosby continued to play the commander role in deciding who would go with whom. This was especially true in the case of Maj. Dolly Richards and Lt. Col. William Chapman. The "tentative" list for the group portraits was William Chapman, Sam Chapman, Stockton Terry, Jim Wiltshire, Adolphus E. "Dolly" Richards, and Fountain Beattie. Peter Franklin, who was to be in the group, had died, but Ben Palmer and John Russell were added.[3]

1. Keen and Mewborn, *43rd Battalion*; John S. Russell was Mosby's scout in the Shenandoah Valley during the war and was one of Mosby's closest friends. Following the war, Russell adopted as his middle name "Singleton," which was Colonel Mosby's name.
2. GLC 3921.50. John Mosby. Autograph letter signed: to Sam Chapman, 19 February 1915 (The Gilder Lehrman Collection, courtesy of The Gilder Lehrman Institute of American History, New York).
3. Mitchell, *Letters*, Otto Walter Beck to John Mosby, January 9, 1915; John Mosby to John Russell, February 17, 1915.

"Rooms for a Dollar a Day"

Colonel Mosby continued to lead the charge, advising Sam Chapman where he could get a room for a dollar a day. The men would travel to New York for the portrait sittings on April 15; Mosby thought the country would be at war with Germany by that date.

———

Febry. 19th 1915   The Alamo, Washington

Dear Sam:

I recd. your letter & sent it to Stockton Terry. I enclose an advertisement of a fine hotel where you can get rooms for a dollar a day. You all had better go there. Send it to Richards (& don't lose it)—You can correspond with Col. Wm. (or Josie)—Richards—Terry—& Ben Palmer & arrange for you all to go on April 15th. By that time we will probably be at war with Germany.

Yours truly
Jno. S. Mosby[1]

———

1. GLC 3921.50. John Mosby. Autograph letter signed: to Sam Chapman, 19 February 1915 (The Gilder Lehrman Collection, courtesy of The Gilder Lehrman Institute of American History, New York).

Mosby Is Painted Again

Colonel Mosby was again in New York, where he gave a talk and sat for the painting.

March 22nd 1915   54 Wall Street

Dear Sam:

I came here by invitation to deliver an address before the Grill Club last Monday evening. I believe it was a success. I'll leave tomorrow. I sat again for the artist—he expects to paint the group next month. I am stopping at the Hotel Breslin—am writing this in the Law Office where Spottswood is employed. He will call on you when you come here.

Yours truly
Jno. S. Mosby[1]

Mosby was in New York portrait sitting, speaking, and visiting with his grandson Spottswood Campbell. It appeared arrangements had been completed for Beck to paint the other Rangers the following month.

1. GLC 3921.39. John Mosby. Autograph letter signed: to Sam Chapman, 22 March 1915 (The Gilder Lehrman Collection, courtesy of The Gilder Lehrman Institute of American History, New York).

"The Curse of the Stuart Family"

The arguments and counter arguments—and Colonel Mosby's defense of General Stuart and the Gettysburg campaign—seemed to have no end. Who told what to whom and who wrote what and when? The accusations had been going back and forth over the last two decades. Colonel Mosby discussed the correspondence he had with General

Stuart's widow; he also voiced his disgust with Henry Stuart—then Governor Henry Stuart—over his non-reaction to Mosby's writing of the Gettysburg campaign and the defense of his uncle, General Stuart.

June 10th 1915   The Alamo, Washington

Dear Sam:

Your letter recd. I have finished with Beck—have posed twice for him in New York. I shall have nothing to do with selecting a place for the group. You are mistaken in saying that I exposed in the Eighties, McClellan's[1] attempt to suppress evidence in favor of Stuart. I forbore to do so on Mrs. Stuart's account. I was provoked to write her this letter by a letter she endorsed to me from McClellan in wch. he had the impertinence to claim the benefit of what I had done in defense of Stuart. In her letter to me she spoke very kindly of McClellan. I felt indignant & replied to it. I sent both her letter & McClellan's to her to give to McCabe & asked him to give them all to Gov. Stuart wch. he did. Stuart knows all about McClellan's treachery but the family are afraid of the Lee superstition. I told Arthur Clarke—who is a cousin to my children—all about Henry Stuart having urged me to write my book—yet had never written me a line about it—nor even mentioned it when we met. A few months ago Arthur met Stuart & told him what I said. No doubt he was ashamed. To make atonement he wrote me the letter I enclose. My book was published over seven years ago—he has just [illegible]. I wrote Dolly that he didn't understand the curse of the Stuart family. He knew it was fear that kept them silent. To please me Stuart appointed Arthur Clarke to represent him this month at the unveiling of the Gen. Green monument in North Carolina. Read Beauregard's letter again in the Preface to my book. You will see it was written 11 years before my book was published. It does not, as you say, express his opinion of my book but of my article in *Belford* that had the records that McClellan got Mrs. Stuart to try to persuade me to suppress. It was the most infamous act of treachery on his part. Return (don't lose) Stuart's letter.

Yours truly

Jno. S. Mosby[2]

The harsh language Mosby used when speaking of Major McClellan revealed his deep dislike of him. The reason was apparently McClellan's dealings with Mrs. Stuart and his attempts to have material, favorable to Stuart but reflecting unfavorably on Gen. R. E. Lee, suppressed. When McClellan did reveal this material, he took it as his own discovery, although it was nine years after Mosby had written about it in a *Century Magazine* article dated February 9, 1887,[3] and again in an article in the same publication on August 24, 1897. Colonel Mosby had some misgivings relating to his dealings with the artist Otto Walter Beck. Mosby's statement about "a place for the group" was not specific—it was unclear whether he was speaking about a place for the group to be painted or a place for the portraits to be displayed. In any regard he was not to be involved.

1. Maj. Henry McClellan was adjutant to General Stuart and wrote a biography of the general after the war. He was a first cousin to Gen. George B. McClellan, who twice commanded the Union Army of the Potomac.

2. Horace Mewborn Collection; John S. Mosby to Capt. Sam Chapman, June 10 (?), 1915.

3. Mitchell, *Letters*, 219–22, John Mosby to Mrs. General J. E. B. Stuart, June 15, 1915.

Lost Letters

In this short note Colonel Mosby chastised Sam Chapman for what he believed was an apparent lost letter, enclosed with the previous letter written to Sam on June 10. And he inquired about the artist, Beck.

June 18th 1915   Washington

Dear Sam:

A week ago I wrote to you & enclosed a letter from Governor Stuart & asked you to return it immediately. As I have no answer from you I fear that you have lost it—although I warned you not to lose it. I expect to go to Berkeley Springs July 1st & spend a couple of weeks. I hope the water may be of some benefit to my bladder trouble. How are you & Dolly getting along with Beck?

Yours truly

Jno. S. Mosby[1]

In Colonel Mosby's previous letter to Sam Chapman, dated June 10, he had requested Sam to return an enclosed letter written by Governor Stuart, with the admonition not to lose it. Then, eight days later, Mosby wrote Chapman that he feared he had lost it. If the date of the previous letter was, in fact, June 10, it appeared the Colonel was allowing sufficient time for Sam to receive his mail and reply. However, the date on the previous letter may have been June 16, not June 10. As there was no postal cover, the mail date is not actually known, but the date written by Colonel Mosby looked to be June 16 and not June 10. (The earlier date is used solely because Mosby says in this letter, dated June 18, "A week ago I wrote to you.") In keeping with his normal itinerary, Colonel Mosby was again going to one of the springs resorts. This time it was in West Virginia, about thirty miles north of Winchester, Virginia. The artist Beck was still on his mind even though he had previously stated, "I have finished with Beck."[2]

1. GLC 3921.51. John Mosby. Autograph letter signed: to Sam Chapman, 18 June 1915 (The Gilder Lehrman Collection, courtesy of The Gilder Lehrman Institute of American History, New York).

2. Horace Mewborn Collection, John S. Mosby to Capt. Sam Chapman, June 10 [?], 1915.

"Virginians Who Were Union Soldiers"

Mosby wrote that he enjoyed his stay at the springs; he had even seen, for the first time, some Virginians who were Union soldiers. He sent to Beck, the artist, a Charlottesville newspaper with the account of his recent visit there.

June 28th [1915]   Hotel Dunn
Monday   Berkeley Springs, W. Va.

Dear Sam:
    I came here last Friday & shall return to Washington next
Friday. Am drinking freely of the water. I hope it will help
my bladder trouble. There are only a few here now—I never
before saw Virginians who were Union soldiers. They are very
friendly to me. One sent me a handsome bouquet—so I sent
it to my grand daughter, Pauline, by parcel post. It is a great
institution. A large company is expected in July. I hope you all
are getting on well with Beck. I wrote Prof. Kent that Beck wd.
select the place where the painting wd. be put & those in the
group did not want the University to have any expense about
it. I simply sent Beck a Charlottesville paper with an account
of my visit.

                                         Yours truly
                                         Jno. S. Mosby[1]

During the war, elements of Mosby's Forty-third Virginia Cavalry
fought skirmishes against a unit known as the Loudoun Rangers,
composed primarily of Union men from Upper Loudoun County, Virginia. It was organized in 1862 to specifically counteract the various
guerrilla bands then operating in that region.[2] Mosby's command had
not yet been formed; it would be organized the following year. There
were several skirmishes between the two commands but for various
reasons, Mosby himself never took part in any of them—and thus, he
"never saw Virginians who were Union soldiers." The Loudoun Rangers finally met their doom, on April 6, 1865, at the hands of the Forty-
third Battalion's Company H, led by Capt. George Baylor.[3] From the
wording of this letter, it seems that Colonel Mosby might have been
in favor of placing the group painting at the university; however, the
artist Beck had the final say.

    1. GLC 3921.52. John Mosby. Autograph letter signed: to Sam Chap-
man, 28 June [1915] (The Gilder Lehrman Collection, courtesy of The Gilder
Lehrman Institute of American History, New York).

2. Brown, *Mosby's Fighting Parson*, 164.
3. Ibid., 285.

Mosby Grieves for His Son

On August 26, 1915, Colonel Mosby's eldest son, John S. "Johnnie" Mosby Jr., succumbed to throat cancer—the same affliction that claimed Mosby's good friend General Grant some thirty years before. Mosby went into an extended period of grieving and depression, canceling all appointments and refusing to leave the house for several months. When he again corresponded with Sam Chapman he took Sam to task for what he had written—or not written—in his letters to Mosby.

———

January 4th 1916   1440 Rhode Island Avenue
                                    [Washington]

Dear Sam:

Your letter just rec'd. I can't remember of course all the letters I got in my affliction & do not suppose that all who wrote to me expected an answer. Besides if I did not answer that was no reason you couldn't write again. There was a time when you did not stand on such ceremony with me. I am surprised that you did not mention Willie Chapman in your letter. He ought to be to you a more interesting subject—he certainly is to me—than the [illegible] you wrote so much about. Now I got a card announcing Willie's marriage last month to Ms. [No entry] & immediately wrote to him.[1] The card said that they wd. be at home at the Palace Hotel after December 10th. I have no answer from him. Suppose he sent you a card & yet you did not call his name. Fount left Alexandria on Nov. 20th for California; he got back on December 24th—was gone 34 days. As he stopped at Salt Lake & then [illegible] & as the trip to California is 5 days he could not have spent much over a week with Clay[2] who is on a railroad up in Oregon. He had not seen Clay for 28 years.

Why he returned so quickly I can't understand as he is doing nothing at home. As the Negroes used to say he went after a chunk of fire. It has been nearly two years since I had a letter from Col. William. His last letter was devoted to a defense of the Commissioner for dismissing Fount. I hear that Willie had bought you a farm near Covington. I suppose you are living on it. I do hope you are not displeased at his marriage but I am surprised that you did not mention him as you know the interest I feel in him. I heard that Col. William had taken all his family to North Carolina. Is that so? I did not think Josie wd. stay long in Richmond if he was not there. I had a very cordial letter from Emerson Stuart yesterday.

Very truly

Jno. S. Mosby[3]

━━━●●●━━━

Willie Chapman's marriage in December 1915 was as big a surprise to his father as it was to Colonel Mosby. Willie wrote Sam, in a letter dated December 15, saying he "was married Monday."[4] The farm mentioned is the one Willie bought at auction in 1911. Colonel Mosby said he had not heard from Col. William Chapman in "nearly two years"; however, on February 4, 1915—nine months previously—Mosby said: "Colonel Wm. writes that he is willing to go,"[5] referring to the sitting for the group portrait in New York that spring. About the only people Mosby wrote to with any regularity during that period were his grandsons Mosby and Spottswood Campbell.[6]

1. Brown, *Mosby's Fighting Parson*, 253; Willie Chapman married a San Francisco socialite named Ruby in December 1915. The marriage would not last; Willie brought his new bride to Virginia, but she was soon back in San Francisco after seeing the mountain farm where she was to be living.

2. Fount Beattie's son.

3. Stuart-Mosby Historical Society Collection.

4. Brown, *Mosby's Fighting Parson*, 353; letter from Willie Chapman to Papa [Sam Chapman], December 15, 1915.

5. GLC 3921.50. John Mosby. Autograph letter signed: to Sam Chapman, 4 February 1916 (The Gilder Lehrman Collection, courtesy of The Gilder Lehrman Institute of American History, New York).

6. Mitchell, *Letters*, 217–41.

"Nothing from Willie"

Willie Chapman had been married for about two months, and Colonel Mosby lamented his lack of communication. The picture business had been given to Dolly Richards. Col. William Chapman (and Josie) would transfer to San Francisco.

———⋗•⋖———

Febry. 17 1916   1440 Rhode Island Avenue
                                      [Washington]

Dear Sam:

I have just rec'd. your letter addressed to me at The Alamo at wch. I left about a year ago & had almost forgotten that I ever lived there. I have rec'd. nothing from Willie since his marriage except a card announcing it. I really have a curiosity to know where he went. I have written him two letters but have no answer. In your former letter you did not mention him & in the one just rec'd. you speak of his being in San Francisco on the 19th but do not say where he has been hiding wch. is a good deal like your trip to Mt. Vernon on a Sunday when you found the gate locked. I rather suspect from your letter that Willie & his wife are not on this hemisphere. I recd. a magazine with his picture wch. I suppose he sent me wch. I sent to Chinn.[1] It has been a long time since I heard from Beck & I turned the management of the picture business over to Dolly Richards. I had a letter from Col. William—the first in two years—saying that he & Josie were about starting to San Francisco. He has been ordered on duty there. As you do not refer to it I suppose you have not heard of it. I do not think the order was very agreeable to him.[2] I suppose he & Willie will meet. I expect to run down to Norfolk about the middle of March & spend two weeks there in The Sisters Hospital. I think the change to the salt air will do me good. Frazer was to see me yesterday. He is here under a doctor & is in poor health. My observation is that Woodrow will be beaten. If the Republicans nominate Hughes[3] or Root I think that either will carry Va. Frazer told me he thought so.

Very truly, Jno. S. Mosby[4]

Mosby thought that President Wilson would be beaten, probably believing that Wilson could not keep the United States out of war before the elections in nine months. He also believed that the Republicans would nominate either Charles Evans Hughes, former governor of New York and then an associate justice of the U.S. Supreme Court, or Elihu Root, former U.S. senator from New York and winner of the Nobel Peace Prize in 1912. The Colonel looked with anticipation on his trip to Norfolk; he seemed to relish the springs and the salt air and water—he always felt better after partaking!

1. Siepel, *Rebel*, 247; Keen and Mewborn, *43rd Battalion*, 306 (roster); Benton Chinn was a former Ranger and friend of Mosby, living in Alexandria, Virginia.
2. Col. William Chapman was transferred to San Francisco prior to his retiring in Greensboro, North Carolina.
3. Charles Evans Hughes was the Republican candidate in 1916, losing the election to the incumbent president Woodrow Wilson.
4. Stuart-Mosby Historical Society Collection.

Taking Charge of Beck

It seemed that the artist Beck was still on Mosby's mind regardless of what he said about his non-association with him. He was greatly looking forward to his trip to Norfolk and was still upset at not hearing anything from Willie Chapman.

Febry. 27th 1916   1440 Rhode Island Avenue

Dear Sam:

You & Dolly Richards must take charge of Beck & his picture. I have been suffering a good deal this winter with my bladder trouble but am much better now & have confidence to go down to Norfolk & spend some time in St. Vincent's Hospital—think the climate & salt air will do a great deal toward restoring me. So on Sunday evening, March 12th, I shall take the Norfolk boat & shall be there in the next morning. I hope to have a pleasant time with the Sisters of the hospital. It is said to be a nice place & I expect to go on some excursions around the country. I have a few acquaintances there. I have written three times to Willie since I rec'd card announcing his marriage but no answer. Has he left the Japanese S.S. Co.? I have heard they wd. employ him in San Francisco.

Yours truly
Jno. S. Mosby[1]

It is difficult to know just what sort of problems the men had with the artist Otto Walter Beck. References within many of Mosby's letters seem to indicate a problem there. The other thing on Mosby's mind, besides his health, was Willie Chapman. Mosby felt very close to Sam's boy—"I feel towards him as if he were my son,"[2] he had written on one occasion—and it was difficult for him to understand Willie's lack of communication with him. But Mosby did not seem to take into account the fact that Willie was in love and had just gotten married. The other thing he did not know was that Willie had left the sea and was looking for a job on land in San Francisco. "The sea has no attraction at all for me now that I am married and never has had for Ruby,"[3] he wrote his father.

1. GLC 3921.54. John Mosby. Autograph letter signed: to Sam Chapman, 27 February 1916 (The Gilder Lehrman Collection, courtesy of The Gilder Lehrman Institute of American History, New York).
2. Brown, *Mosby's Fighting Parson*, 322.
3. Ibid., 354, letter from Willie Chapman to Papa [Sam Chapman], March 10, 1916.

"He Now Has No Further Use for Me"

Mosby was at a hospital in Norfolk where he was able to take in the salt air but he reflected inwardly upon his relationship with Willie Chapman. He had not heard from him since Willie's marriage the previous December and Willie had not responded to his letters. The Colonel took this to mean he had no further use for him.

March 16th 1916   St. Vincent's Hospital and Sanitarium
                         Norfolk, Va.

Dear Sam:

The only news I have had from Willie is a card announcing
his marriage & a pamphlet with his picture wch. I sent to
Chinn. I have written to him three times since I got the card—
no answer—as my letters were not returned to me he must
have recd. them. I suppose he now has no further use for me.
I came here last Monday—have been kindly treated but so far
have kept in the house. Dr. Lynch who is attending me says he
can cure me. I expect to stay several weeks—hope to get back
well. The Sisters take good care of me. In a few days I shall call
on Mrs. General Stuart & Will Brooke.[1] If the latter were well
I wd. not go to see him. He is now a wreck. You seem from
your letter very much afraid that you will write me something.
A storm is raging on the coast—when it is over I shall run over
to Va. Beach. Was Col. William banished to the Pacific Coast?
How does Josie like it? I came here for the mild weather but
have run into a blizzard. But it will only last a day. I suppose
Col. Wm. will stay in California until close of Woodrow's term
next March. If he is nominated he will carry Va.

                                        Yours truly
                                        Jno. S. Mosby[2]

Just got a phone [call] from Mrs. General Stuart asking me to
dine with her tomorrow.

———

Willie Chapman's failure to answer Colonel Mosby's letters left the old
veteran heartsick and with a feeling of obsolescence. And Sam Chapman apparently was not writing anything of import—or so thought
Mosby—which served to further amplify his general despondency.
Less than two weeks before this letter from John Mosby, Sam Chapman had received one from his brother William, newly arrived in San
Francisco. William told Sam that he had received a copy of a letter
written by the artist Otto Walter Beck to Dolly Richards, relative to

the painting of the group of Mosby's men.[3] The sittings for the paintings were to have been accomplished a year previously but apparently this had not been the case. Mosby had twice sat, the last time being sometime before June 10, 1915.[4] It is not known who else may have been painted for the group, if any. Certainly Colonel William had not been, from what he tells Sam in his March 5, 1916, letter. Beck had wanted William to come to the small village of Pelham Manor, about fifteen miles from New York city, but as William explained in his letter to Sam, "I am so far off now that it would be impossible for me to get to Pelham Manor but I will write to Mr. Beck & send him a photograph of myself taken during the war which Josie has kept & brought with her." This was followed by some skepticism on the part of William, which might help to explain the dubious feelings shown at times by Colonel Mosby, relative to Beck. William Chapman wrote, "If I thought the artist's work on the canvas would equal his descriptions with the pen I could have more faith in his undertaking." As to the location of the finished work, William wrote that he "would prefer seeing it at the Univ. of Va. to any other place that it could be placed in."[5]

1. Keen & Mewborn, *43rd Battalion,* 301 (roster). William T. Brooke served under Mosby during the war. He had graduated with honors from the University of Virginia and was Mosby's vice-consul to Hong Kong between 1879 and 1881. He was later city engineer of Norfolk, Virginia. It is unknown why Mosby considered him "a wreck."

2. GLC 3921.55. John Mosby. Autograph letter signed: to Sam Chapman, 16 March 1916 (The Gilder Lehrman Collection, courtesy of The Gilder Lehrman Institute of American History, New York).

3. Charles Lewis Collection, Letter from W. H. Chapman to S. F. Chapman, March 5, 1916.

4. Horace Mewborn Collection, Letter from Jno. S. Mosby to Capt. Sam Chapman, June 10 or 16, 1915.

5. Charles Lewis Collection, Letter from W. H. Chapman to S. F. Chapman, March 5, 1916.

"The Final Word"

Sam Chapman had been talking to a news dealer regarding a lecture by Colonel Mosby. "It will be the final word on Stuart & Gettysburg."

April 10th 1916   1440 Rhode Island Avenue
                                                   Washington

Dear Sam:

   Your letter recd. You say that the news dealer wrote to
the *North American Review* for a copy of it with my Quill
Club lecture. I did not write you that it had been published
but that it had been accepted. It may be published in six
months. You ask the price of the *Review.* The news dealer can
tell you. When they put it in print they will send me proofs
of it for corrections & then inform me when it will appear.
I have not been taking any interest in Beck's paintings. The
lecture is a great improvement on my book & I think it will
be the final word on Stuart & Gettysburg. I think Woodrow's
Administration will close next March.

                                                   Your truly
                                                   Jno. S. Mosby[1]

Mosby had been back in Washington about a week after spending
three weeks in Norfolk and took Sam to task over the publication of
a magazine article. He was soon in Georgetown University Hospital
and by May 11 was in Garfield Hospital, and as one of his daughters
wrote to a friend, "There is reason to think he will ultimately entirely
recover."[2] Col. John Singleton Mosby died May 30, 1916.

   1. (Copy) Peter A. Brown Collection.
   2. Siepel, *Rebel*, 291, Stuart (Mosby) Coleman to Lena N. Haxall, May
11, 1916.

Conclusion

It is not known if there were more letters from John Mosby to Sam Chapman following the one of April 10, 1916. Seven weeks later, on May 30, Mosby died in Garfield Hospital, Washington, D.C. He was eighty-two years, six months old. The cause of death has been attributed to several different maladies, from an enlarged and inflamed prostate, to a toxicity of the urinary tract, to a general debility. The old veteran probably suffered from them all, however his certificate of death, only recently located after having been "missing" for years, gives the official cause of death as a malignant neoplasm (growth) of the liver.[1] It is ironic that he survived so many injurious blows—wounded at least three times by bullets, one of which he carried for the rest of his life; injured several times by falling mounts and tree limbs; victim of a skull fracture from being kicked by a horse that left him minus an eye—only to die at an advanced age in a hospital room.

The dealing that was going on—and off—between the artist Otto Walter Beck and John Mosby mentioned in several letters would eventually be completed, and at least partly in the manner envisioned originally. In the end there would be a triptych consisting of Colonel Mosby, Dr. William L. Dunn, and Lt. Charles Edward Grogan in the center panel; Lt. Fountain Beattie, Lt. Frank Henry Rahm, and Lt. John Singleton Russell in the left panel; Dr. James Girard Wiltshire and Maj. Adolphus Edward "Dolly" Richards in the right panel. Notably missing were Capt. Samuel Forrer Chapman, Lt. Col. William Henry Chapman, Pvt. and Color Bearer Robert Stockton Terry, and Lt. William Benjamin "Ben" Palmer. William Chapman had transferred to San Francisco and could not come to New York to sit. According to Colonel Mosby's letter of April 16, 1915, Sam Chapman and Stockton

Terry were to leave the following night for New York to sit for the artist, so the result of their scheduled trip is a mystery.

Otto Walter Beck was born near Dayton, Ohio, on March 11, 1864. His imagination kindled by the stories he heard of the war from old veterans at the local soldier's home, he became determined to make a series of paintings as a memorial to these men. The result was the life-sized paintings of veterans, both North and South, grouped according to regiments. In addition to the Mosby groups, he painted the "Old Guard of New York" and the New York Volunteer Infantry, the Duryee Zouaves (The Fighting Fifth). It is unknown where the Mosby Triptych was initially placed, but eventually it found a home at the National Museum of American Art, Smithsonian Institution. On May 22, 1999, Beck's works were sold at auction in Washington, D.C. Each panel of the Mosby Triptych was sold individually.

As for his *Memoirs*, Colonel Mosby did not live to see it in print. However, the work was edited and publication secured by his brother-in-law Charles Wells Russell in 1917, the year after Mosby's death.

On the day of Mosby's funeral, June 1, 1916, in Warrenton, twenty-seven members of his old command were there serving as bodyguard and pallbearers; Sam Chapman, standing tall, with neatly trimmed white beard, mustache, and full head of hair, was counted. As his old commander and friend was laid beneath the cool Virginia soil, was it possible that Sam remembered a line from one of Mosby's letters, when the Colonel was making plans to travel from California to Virginia to see him: "I would prefer to reach there in the daytime or early in the night," he had confided, "as I have a horror of being waked up at night"?[2]

In late September 1918, the rapidly diminishing group of "Mosby's Men" united in Front Royal on the fifty-fourth anniversary of the brutal execution there of six of their command by Union cavalry. They had been led that fateful day, so long ago, by Capt. Sam Chapman, and now he was there again, once more to pay homage to them and to meet for the last time those with whom he had ridden. Eight months later, on May 21, 1919, Sam Chapman passed away, just nine days prior to the three-year anniversary of Mosby's death.

1. Certificate of Death, District of Columbia Department of Health, Vital Records Division.

2. Kincheloe Collection; Letter from John Mosby to Sam Chapman, November 28, 1894.

Bibliography

Published Sources

Brown, Peter A. "Confederates in Vermont—A Mosby Connection." *Southern Cavalry Review,* Vol. 21, No. 3. Lancaster, Pa.: Stuart-Mosby Historical Society, 2003.

———. *Mosby's Fighting Parson: The Life and Times of Sam Chapman.* Westminster, Md.: Willow Bend Books, 2001.

Carmichael, Peter S. *Lee's Young Artillerist: William J. Pegram.* Charlottesville: University Press of Virginia, 1995.

Chaitkin, Anton. *Lincoln by Anton Chaitkin.* Washington, D.C.: Schiller Institute, 1998.

Coulter, E. Merton. *A History of the South.* Vol. 7, *The Confederate States of America.* Baton Rouge: Louisiana State University Press, 1950.

Faust, Patricia L., ed. *Historical Times Illustrated Encyclopedia of the Civil War.* New York: Harper and Row Publishers, 1986.

Freeman, Douglas Southall. *Lee's Lieutenants: A Study in Command.* 3 vols. New York: Charles Scribner's Sons, 1942.

Haselberger, Fritz. *Confederate Retaliation: McCausland's 1864 Raid.* Shippensburg, Pa.: Burd Street Press, 2000.

Headley, John. *Confederate Operations in Canada and New York.* Neale Publishing Company, 1906.

Heinemann, Ronald I. *Harry Byrd of Virginia.* Charlottesville: University Press of Virginia, 1996.

Jones, Virgil Carrington. *Ranger Mosby.* Chapel Hill: University Press of North Carolina, 1944.

Keen, Hugh C., and Horace Mewborn. *43rd Battalion/Virginia Cavalry/ Mosby's Command.* Lynchburg, Va.: H. E. Howard, Inc. 1993.

Lee, Fitzhugh. *General Lee,* 1899. New York: D. Appleton and Co.

Lowery, Terry D. *22nd Virginia Infantry.* The Virginia Regimental History Series. Lynchburg, Va.: H. E. Howard, Inc., 1988.

McKim, Randolph Harrison. *A Soldier's Recollections.* New York: Longmans, Green, and Co., 1910.

Mewborn, Horace, ed. *"From Mosby's Command: Newspaper Articles by and about John S. Mosby and His Raiders."* Baltimore, Md.: Butternut and Blue, 2005.

Mitchell, Adele H., ed. *The Letters of John S. Mosby, 2nd ed.* Stuart-Mosby Historical Society, 1986.

Mitchell, Lt. Col. Joseph B. Jr., *Decisive Battles of the Civil War.* New York: G. P. Putnam's Sons, 1955.

Mosby, John S. *The Memoirs of Colonel John S. Mosby.* Ed. by Charles Wells Russell. Boston: Little, Brown and Co., 1917.

———. *Mosby's War Reminiscences and Stuart's Cavalry Campaigns.* New York: Dodd Mead and Company, 1887. Facsimile Reprint Edition, Harrisburg, Pa.: Archive Society, 1995.

———. *Stuart's Cavalry in the Gettysburg Campaign.* New York: Moffat, Yard and Company, 1908.

Munson, John W. *Reminiscences of a Mosby Guerrilla.* New York: Moffat, Yard and Company, 1906.

Ramage, James A. *Gray Ghost.* Lexington: University Press of Kentucky, 1999.

Reader's Digest Association. *The Family Encyclopedia of American History.* Pleasantville, N.Y.: 1975.

Scott, J. L. *36th Virginia Infantry.* The Virginia Regimental Histories Series. Lynchburg, Va.: H. E. Howard, Inc., 1987.

Scott, Major John. *Partisan Life with Col. John S. Mosby.* New York: Harper and Brothers, Publishers, 1867. Reprint, Gaithersburg, Md.: Olde Soldier Books, Inc., n.d.

Siepel, Kevin. *Rebel: The Life and Times of John Singleton Mosby.* New York: St. Martin's Press, 1983.

Stiles, Kenneth L. *4th Virginia Cavalry.* The Virginia Regimental Histories Series. Lynchburg, Va.: H. E. Howard, Inc., 1985.

Tucker, Robert Dennard. *The Descendants of William Tucker of Throwleigh, Devon.* Washington, D.C.: Schiller Institute, 1998.

U.S. War Department. *War of the Rebellion: A Compilation of the Official Records of the Union and Confederate Armies,* 128 vols. Washington, D.C.: U.S. Government Printing Office, 1880–1901.

Weaver, Jeffrey C. *64th Virginia Infantry.* The Virginia Regimental Histories Series. Lynchburg, Va.: H. E. Howard, Inc., 1992.

Wert, Jeffry D. *Mosby's Rangers.* New York: Simon and Schuster, 1990.

Williamson, James J. *Mosby's Rangers*. New York: Ralph B. Kenyon, Publisher, 1896. 2nd ed. New York: Sturgis and Walton, 1909.

Woodward, Howard R. Jr., *The Confederacy's Forgotten Son, Major General James Lawson Kemper, C.S.A.* Natural Bridge, Va.: Rockbridge Publishing Company, 1993.

Institutional Repositories

Commonwealth of Virginia, Department of Health, Division of Vital Records, Richmond: Death Records of County of Bedford, 1913

District of Columbia, Department of Health, Vital Records Division: Certificates of Death, 1916

Duke University Rare Book, Manuscript, & Special Collections Library, Durham, North Carolina

The Gilder Lehrman Institute of American History, New York

National Archives and Records Administration, Washington, D.C., Compiled Service Records of the Union and the Confederacy

The Schiller Institute, Washington, D.C.

Winchester-Frederick Historical Society, Winchester, Virginia

Newspapers and Periodicals

Alexandria Gazette
New York Herald
New York Times
New York World
Richmond Dispatch
Richmond Times
Richmond Times-Dispatch
San Francisco Call
San Francisco Morning Call
Southern Cavalry Review
Washington Times

Electronic Sources

Biographical Directory of the United States Congress, http://www.congressbioguide.congress.gov

Brief Biography of Bennett H. Young, http://www.wtv-zone.com/civilwar/by.html

Chargers, Specifications against [Lincoln Conspirators], http://www. surratt.org/documents/dcharges.html

Members of The Virginia Convention of 1861: http://www.members. aol.com/jweaver

Mrs. Felicia Dorethea Hemens (1794–1825), The Tyrolesse Evening Hymn (1828): Public Domain Music, http://www.pdmusic.org/ hymns

St. Albans Raid: http://www.wtv-zone.com/civilwar/stalbans.html

Tales of Peter Parley about America: http://www.americanwebbooks. com/book

U.S. Histories, Biographies Encyclopedia: http://reference.allrefer.com/ encyclopedia/

Private Collections

Joe Bauman, Salt Lake City, Utah

Peter A. Brown, Lexington, Virginia

Milton Cockrell, Culpeper, Virginia

Robert M. Daly, Middleburg, Virginia

Fauquier Historical Society, Warrenton, Virginia

The Gilder Lehrman Institute of American History, New York

Dave Goetz, Warrenton, Virginia

Hugh Keen, Tulsa, Oklahoma

John T. Kincheloe, Fairfax, Virginia

Charles Lewis, Buies Creek, North Carolina

Michael Macdonald, Warrenton, Virginia

Horace Mewborn, New Bern, North Carolina

The John Singleton Mosby Foundation, Inc., Warrenton, Virginia

Stuart-Mosby Historical Society, Lancaster, Pennsylvania

Virginia Baptist Historical Society, Richmond, Virginia

Index

Alger, Col. Russell A. (U.S.), 36,
    37n3
Allen, Brown, 49, 54, 55–56
Army of Northern Virginia
    (C.S.), 1, 2, 80
Arthur, Chester A. (President),
    22, 62n3

Baldwin, John Brown, 76, 77n4,
    93, 93n3, 100
Barton, Capt. (U.S.), 56–57
Baylor, Capt. George (C.S.), 145
Beattie, Clay, 33, 33n7, 146–47
Beattie, Ernest, 33, 33n7
Beattie, Fountain, "Fount"
    (C.S.), 3–4, 5n14, 15,
    32–33, 33n2, 33n7, 52, 53,
    82, 83n1, 114, 116–17,
    117n2, 125, 126, 126n7,
    127, 127n2, 130–31, 132,
    133, 139–40, 146–47,
    147n2, 155
Beck, Otto Walter, 126n2,
    140n3, 141–45, 148–53, 155,
    156
Bedford, Va., 51, 62, 63, 64,
    73n2, 76, 81, 85, 86n1, 87,
    88, 97, 108, 111–12, 117n15
Berkeley Springs, W.Va., 144,
    145

Berryville, Va., 12, 38–39, 39n8,
    43, 83 (see also Front Royal
    executions)
Bispham, Lt. Stacy Budd (C.S.),
    76, 77n6
Blazer, Col. Richard (U.S.), 24,
    26, 28, 31, 40
Blazer's Scouts (U.S.), 16, 24,
    25n7, 26, 28, 31, 40, 41n2
Brady, James D., 34, 35n4
Bristol, Va., 1, 86, 87, 94, 114
Brooke, James V. Jr., 22, 23n4
Brooke, Pvt. William T. (C.S.),
    151, 152n1
Bryan, Pvt. Joseph (C.S.), 28, 37,
    39, 41, 54, 54n4, 60, 61–62,
    72, 73n1, 86, 87–88

Calhoun, John C., 74, 75n4
Campbell, May Mosby
    (daughter), 70n3, 88n2
Campbell, Mosby (grandson), 3,
    69, 88, 121, 122, 147
Campbell, Spottswood
    (grandson), 3, 69, 87, 88,
    115, 121, 139, 141, 147
Century Magazine, 143
Chapman, Elgin (son), 15, 45
Chapman, Mary (daughter), 55,
    122n1

Chapman, Rebecca (wife), 15, 17, 45–46

Chapman, William Allen, "Willie" (son), 3, 4, 11, 13–17, 23, 24, 25n4, 26, 28, 29, 31, 32–33, 33n7, 34, 41, 42, 44, 45n2, 51, 64, 69, 76–77, 85, 88, 109, 111, 130, 135, 136, 147, 147n1, 148–50

Chapman, Lt. Col. William Henry, "Col. William" (brother, C.S.), 5n4, 26, 28, 30, 31, 38, 39, 39n8, 41, 43n5, 45n5, 47, 50, 52, 67, 83, 92, 94, 115, 127, 128, 132, 134, 137, 139, 140, 147–48, 149n2, 151, 155

Charlottesville, Va., 35, 76, 81n4, 115n2, 136–37, 138n2, 144

Charlottesville Progress, 70, 145

"Children of the Mist," 43n6, 44n11

Chinn, Pvt. Benton (C.S.), 65, 66n1, 148, 149n1, 151

Christian, Judge George L., 73–74, 75n1, 79

Cleveland, Grover (President), 22, 26, 33, 52

Coleman, Virginia Stuart Mosby (daughter), 23, 25n2, 26, 28, 29n3, 79, 115n3, 116, 118, 118n5, 119, 153n2

Covington, Va., 4, 14, 18, 26, 28, 36, 41, 42, 55, 103, 121, 131, 133, 147

Covington Baptist Church, 4, 14, 18, 23, 34, 45, 51, 72

Cuba, 2, 14–15, 36, 37, 48, 49, 122, 123

Custer, Gen. George A. (U.S.), 12, 29, 29n4, 37, 38, 39nn7–8, 41, 43, 43n1, 83, 133–35

Daniel, Maj. John W. (C.S.), 15, 36, 45, 45n4, 46–49, 51–53, 55, 83, 85, 86

Davis, Jefferson, 71, 74, 78–80, 89, 91, 95, 100–101

Dunn, Dr. William L. (C.S.), 116, 119, 155

Emerson, Ralph Waldo, 57, 59nn5–6, 106

Ferguson, Pvt. Sydnor Gilbert, "Syd" (C.S.), 30, 31, 32n2

Forbes, Maj. William H. (U.S.), 11–13, 57, 59n4, 106, 107, 107n5, 124

Forty-third Battalion (C.S.), 1, 2, 16, 25n5, 33n2, 62n2, 71n4, 137–38, 145

Free silver/gold standard debate, 32–33, 33n5, 34–35 (*see also* Gold standard/free silver debate)

Front Royal executions, 2, 29, 37, 39, 41–43, 43n1, 133, 135, 156 (*see also* Berryville, Va.)

Fugitive Slave Law, 74–75

Garfield, James (President), 21, 22

Gettysburg, Pa., 11, 54, 55–56, 76–77, 84, 85, 87, 96, 99, 111, 101–2, 103, 104, 107, 115–16, 118, 121, 132, 141–42

Gold standard/free silver debate, 26, 32–33, 33n5 (*see also*

Free silver/gold standard debate) Gordon, Armistead, 70, 71, 71n2, 71n4, 76, 77, 79, 89, 91, 102
Grant, Capt. Fred (U.S.), 92, 92n3,
Grant, Gen. Ulysses S. (U.S., President), 2, 13, 22, 38, 39, 42, 43, 43n6, 47, 56, 57, 60, 66, 70, 75n3, 78, 79, 91, 92, 121n1, 127, 133–35, 146
Grant, U. S. III, 114
Greeley, Horace, 74, 75n3
Greenback Raid, 16, 68, 81, 81n2
Grogan, Lt. Charles Edward (C.S.), 155
Guatemala mission, 34, 35n2

Hanna, Mark, 34, 35, 35n3, 42
Harper's Weekly, 26, 28, 31
Hayes, Rutherford B. (President), 21, 22, 27, 27n7, 127
"Headless horseman," 69, 70, 72, 100, 101n3 (see also McIlhany, Hugh)
Heth, Gen. George Henry (C.S.), 77, 77n8, 101–2, 102n1
Hill, Gen. Ambrose Powell (C.S.), 76–77, 77nn7–8, 99, 101–2, 129
Hitchcock, Ethan Allen, 47–49 (see also U.S. Department of the Interior)
Hitchcock, Frank H., 108
Hong Kong, 2, 4, 21, 22, 23, 29, 31, 34, 38, 44, 106–7, 109, 139, 152n1
Hunter, Maj. Robert (C.S.), 63, 64n4

Huntington, C. P., 47 (see also Southern Pacific Railroad)

Internal Revenue Service, 2, 35n4, 45, 82, 83, 126, 132

Jackson, Gen. Thomas J., "Stonewall" (C.S.), 77n7, 111, 112, 129
James, Jesse, 32
Jeffries, Josie (Mrs. William H. Chapman), 16, 30, 42, 43n5, 45, 46–47, 49–50, 68, 70, 88, 113, 116, 118, 125, 128, 134, 135, 137, 139, 140, 147, 148, 151–52
Jeffries, Mrs., 32, 42, 43n5, 68–69
Johnson, Andrew (President), 78–80, 91, 135

Keith, Judge James, 66, 79, 80n3, 83, 100, 118, 118n4

Lady Astor (Nancy Langhorne), 114–15, 115n1, 118, 118n4
Lee, Gen. Fitzhugh, "Fitz" (C.S.), 40, 41, 108
Lee, Gen. Robert E. (C.S.), 1, 2, 12, 25, 37–38, 40, 54–55, 57, 60, 76–77, 78, 80, 82, 85, 96–99, 102, 104, 107, 119, 128–30, 142, 143
Leslie's Illustrated Newspaper, 45n3
Leslie's Weekly, 106, 107n2
Lincoln, Abraham (President), 74, 79, 88, 89, 95
Long, Col. Armistead L. (C.S.), 76, 77
Longstreet, Gen. James (C.S.), 16, 55–56, 129

Loudoun Rangers (U.S.), 145
Lynchburg, Va., 76, 81, 82–83,
    85–87, 90, 97, 98n1, 115n1,
    118n4

Marshall, Col. Charles (C.S.),
    76–77, 85, 102
McCabe, Capt. Gordon (C.S.),
    54, 54n4, 60, 142
McCue, Pvt. John (C.S.), 91–92
McDowell, Judge Henry Clay,
    83, 85, 86n2, 90–93, 94, 96,
    98n1
McIlhany, Sgt. Hugh (C.S.), 16,
    58, 60, 65n3, 67, 68n3, 94,
    98, 101n3, 135, 137 (*see also*
    "Headless Horseman")
McKim, Rev. Randolph
    Harrison, 96–98, 98n3, 99,
    103
McKinley, William (President),
    34–35, 35n3, 44, 46, 47, 49,
    53
*The Memoirs of Colonel John
    S. Mosby,* 5n1, 30, 41n5, 81,
    116, 131, 132, 156
Merritt, Gen. Wesley (U.S.), 12,
    38, 39n7, 135
Miles, Gen. Nelson A. (U.S.),
    36–37
Miskel Farm fight, 10, 44–45,
    45n3, 103
Mosby, Beverly, "Bev" (son), 26,
    27n4, 60, 60n1, 64, 83
Mosby, John Jr., "Johnnie"
    (son), 26, 146
Mosby, Lt. William, "Willie"
    (brother, C.S.), 7, 51, 85,
    86n1, 96, 98n2, 108, 111,
    116, 128, 136n3
Mosby triptych, 155–56

Mosby's command, 5n3, 25n2,
    29n2, 68n3, 95n2, 95n6,
    110, 119, 133, 135, 138, 145
Mosby's Hussars, 37
Mosby's men, 37, 39n8, 43,
    44n11, 68, 71, 103, 126,
    128, 152, 156
Mosby's Rangers, 2, 9, 14, 33n2,
    45n3, 59n4, 107n5, 116n1,
    137
Munsey's Magazine, 107
Munson, Maj. John (C.S.), 28,
    29n2, 31, 32, 81

Northern Neck (of Va.), 13,
    24–25, 25n6, 92

Old Dominion Sun, 49, 64
Once a Week, 32
Osborne, William H., 126–27,
    127n1, 130–33

Palmer, Lt. William Benjamin,
    "Ben" (C.S.), 3, 5n14, 62,
    62n2, 63, 64n3, 72, 139,
    140, 155
Payne, Alexander, "Alek," 66,
    67n5, 80n3, 100
Peters, Col. William E. (C.S.),
    42, 43n4
Political patronage, 2, 13, 15,
    44, 51, 53, 105, 113, 120,
    126
Proclamation of Pardon, 72, 78,
    80, 100

Quantrill, William Clarke, 134,
    136n1, 138

Rahm, Lt. Frank Henry (C.S.),
    155

Rangers (C.S.), 9, 11–12, 14, 16, 23, 37, 39, 40, 59n1, 81nn2–3, 83, 125, 141
Reconstruction Committee, 67n4, 76–77, 100
Revercomb, George A., 35, 35n6, 49, 50, 50n3, 51, 97–98, 108, 129, 134, 136
Revercomb, Lizzie Chapman (daughter), 35n6
Richards, Maj. A. E., "Dolly" (C.S.), 13, 24, 25, 25n5, 25n7, 31, 33n4, 41–42, 43, 43n1, 44n11, 115, 116n1, 119, 133, 134–35, 136–37, 140, 148, 149, 151, 155
Richards, Capt. Thomas W. (C.S.), 13, 24, 25, 25n5, 25n7, 31, 33n4, 40, 41nn1–2, 45n7
Richmond, Va., 62n2, 63, 63n1, 64n3, 73, 75, 78, 88, 96, 97, 107, 111, 122n1, 147
Richmond Times-Dispatch, 27n5, 35n4, 36, 37n3, 39, 39n1, 39n8, 43n1, 43n6, 44n10, 54, 60, 73, 73n1, 87, 92n2, 98n4, 108n7
Roosevelt, Theodore, "Teddy" (President), 49–50, 54n1, 69n2, 83, 112nn3–4, 113
Root, Elihu, 47–48, 111, 112n6, 148–49
Rosser, Gen. Thomas L. (C.S.), 28, 29, 29n4
Russell, Charles Wells, 5n1, 41n5, 105, 121n3, 156
Russell, Jack, 115, 120, 121n3, 125, 139
Russell, Lt. John Singleton, (C.S.), 3, 5n14, 139, 140, 140n1, 155

San Francisco Call, 23, 24, 25n10, 35n7, 36, 37n4
Secession, 72, 74, 88–89, 92–93, 93nn2–3, 100
Sheridan, Gen. Phillip (U.S.), 12, 25n7, 27–29, 30, 41–42, 43nn1–3, 43n6, 83, 88, 135
Shipp, Scott (C.S.), 60, 67, 70
Slavery, 73–75, 79, 88, 100–101
Smith, Col. Tom (C.S.), 63, 63n1, 64–65, 66, 100
Smith, Gen. William, "Extra Billy" (C.S.), 23, 63, 63n1, 65, 66, 78–79, 82–83
"Solid South," 26
Southern Pacific Railroad, 2, 23, 47 (see also Huntington, C. P.)
Staunton, Va., 2, 4, 16, 50nn1–2, 54n2, 55, 64, 64nn4–5, 65n3, 67, 69, 73, 79, 84, 89, 97, 129, 135
Stuart, Henry, 17, 117, 118n1, 119, 120, 142, 144
Stuart, Gen. James E. B., "Jeb" (C.S.), 1, 5n1, 10, 17, 27n5, 41, 54, 55, 60, 72, 77, 78–79, 85, 96, 97, 98, 98n4, 99, 101, 102, 104, 118n1, 123–24, 129, 141, 142, 143, 143n1, 152, 153
Stuart, Mrs. Flora, 142–43, 151
Stuart's Cavalry in the Gettysburg Campaign (Mosby), 54, 72, 76, 79, 80, 81, 96, 119

Taft, William Howard (President), 84, 86, 88, 90, 92, 94, 111, 113–14, 124, 129, 133
Talcott, Col. T. M. C. (C.S.), 96, 98, 98n4, 99, 102, 104

Taylor, Col. Walter H. (C.S.), 76, 77, 77n2, 104
Terry, Pvt. Stockton Robert (C.S.), 81, 81n3, 85, 86, 87, 90, 139, 140, 155–56
Torbert, Gen. Alfred (U.S.), 11, 12, 38, 39n7, 135

Underwood Constitution, 66, 67n4
University of Virginia, 1, 23, 35, 62, 69, 70–71, 71n1, 75n5, 81, 81n4, 83, 84n3, 88, 91, 92, 92n1, 137n1, 145, 152n1
U.S. consul, Mosby as, 2, 4, 21, 22, 95n7, 110n2, 139, 152n1
U.S. Department of Justice, 2, 17, 49, 59, 69, 69n2, 93, 105, 107, 111, 128n4
U.S. Department of the Interior, 2, 47–48, 49, 51, 52, 69n2, 95n8 (see also Hitchcock, Ethan Allen)
U.S. marshal, Chapman as, 2, 4, 16, 50n1, 54n3, 55, 69, 85, 88, 97

Walker, Gilbert C., 65–66, 90, 99, 100, 101n1
Warrenton, Va., 1, 2, 9, 22, 23n2, 23n4, 28, 63n1, 65, 79, 80n3, 86, 89n3, 90, 100, 102, 113, 114, 117, 118n2, 129, 156
Washington Post, 50, 108, 121
Wilson, Woodrow (President), 4, 112n3, 112n5, 118–19, 120, 121, 123–24, 127n3, 130, 131, 132, 134, 139, 148, 149n3, 151, 153
Wiltshire, Lt. James Girard (C.S.), 76, 77n5, 139–40, 155
Wright, Gen. Marcus (C.S.), 38

Young, Bennett H., 135, 136, 138
Yost, Samuel, 54, 54n2, 55, 56, 58, 60, 61, 62, 63, 64, 65n3, 66, 68, 69, 71, 74, 100